Kenneth R. Pirok

COMMERCIAL LOAN ANALYSIS

Principles and Techniques for Credit Analysts and Lenders

A *BankLine* Publication
PROBUS PUBLISHING COMPANY
Chicago, Illinois
Cambridge, England

BANK LINE™

© 1994, Probus Publishing Company

ALL RIGHTS RESERVED. No part of this publication may be reproduced, stored in a retrieval system, or transmitted, in any form or by any means, electronic, mechanical, photocopying, recording, or otherwise, without the prior written permission of the publisher and the author.

This publication is designed to provide accurate and authoritative information in regard to the subject matter covered. It is sold with the understanding that the author and the publisher are not engaged in rendering legal, accounting, or other professional service.

Authorization to photocopy items for internal or personal use, or the internal or personal use of specific clients, is granted by PROBUS PUBLISHING COMPANY, provided that the U.S. $7.00 per page fee is paid directly to Copyright Clearance Center, 222 Rosewood Drive, Danvers, MA 01923, USA; Phone: 1-508-750-8400. For those organizations that have been granted a photocopy license by CCC, a separate system of payment has been arranged. The fee code for users of the Transactional Reporting Service is 1-55738-716-8/94/$00.00 + $7.00.

ISBN 1-55738-716-8

Printed in the United States of America

IPC

ALT

1 2 3 4 5 6 7 8 9 0

Probus books are available at quantity discounts when purchased for business, educational, or sales promotional use. For more information, please call the Director, Corporate/Institutional Sales at (800) 998-4644, or write:

Director, Corporate/Institutional Sales
Probus Publishing Company
1925 N. Clybourn Avenue
Chicago, IL 60614
PHONE (800) 998-4644   FAX (312) 868-6250

TABLE OF CONTENTS

Acknowledgments vii

Preface ix

**Chapter 1 Introduction to Commercial Loan Analysis:
           A Crucial Bank Function** 1
   Commercial Loan Analysis 1
   Case Study 1

**Chapter 2 Spreading and Analyzing Financial
           Statements** 5
   Spreading 5
   Assets 6
   Liabilities 7
   Income Statement 7
   Analysis of Spreads 8
   Case Study: Charlie's Chocolate Company 10
   Spreading the Financial Statements 16
   Analyzing the Completed Spreads 19

Chapter 3 Ratio Analysis 29
   Liquidity Ratios 29
   Turnover/Activity Ratios 31

Table of Contents

    Leverage Ratios 33
    Coverage Ratios 34
    Profitability/Efficiency/Operating Ratios 37
    Breakeven Ratios 30
    Case Study: Analysis of Charlie's Chocolate Company's
        Ratios 38

Chapter 4 Cash Flow and Debt Service Coverage Analysis 43
    Introduction to Cash Flow 43
    Accrual Basis Cash Flow Calculation 44
    Cash Basis Cash Flow 48
    Cash Basis Cash Flow Calculation 49
    Analysis of Debt Service Coverage 50
    Analysis of Accrual versus Cash Basis 51
    Impacts upon Cash Flow 52
    Analysis of Capital Expenditures 54
    Case Study: Cash Flow Analysis of Charlie's Chocolate
        Company 55

Chapter 5 Assessing Business Plans and Management Ability 59
    Business Plans 59
    Topics That a Business Plan Should Address 60
    Management Ability 61

Chapter 6 Analyzing Projections 63
    Analyzing Projections 63
    Case Study: Financial Projections for Charlie's Chocolate
        Company 64
    Analyzing Projections 65

Chapter 7 Analyzing Personal Financial Statements . . 73
    Personal Financial Statements 73
    Adjusted Net-Worth Calculation 74

Table of Contents

    Calculation of Total Liquid Assets 75
    Case Study: Charles Smith's Personal Financial Statement . . . 75
    Calculation of Adjusted Net Worth 75
    Analysis of Adjusted Net Worth and Total Liquid Assets 78

Chapter 8 Personal Cash Flow Analysis 79
    Introduction 79
    Personal Cash Available Calculation 80
    Case Study: Analyzing Mr. Smith's Personal Tax Return 83
    Detailed Explanation 91
    Personal Cash Flow Calculation 92
    Personal Cash Flow Analysis 93

Chapter 9 Loan Structuring and Definitions 95
    Commercial Loan Facilities 95
    Commercial Loan Types/Reasons for Borrowing 96
    Loan Term and Amortization 97
    Loan Pricing 97
    Collateral 98
    Guarantees 102
    Subordination Requirements 103
    Debt Repayment Restrictions 103
    Other Requirements 104

Chapter 10 Sample Loan Presentation 105
    Memorandum 105
    Commercial Loan Analysis—Process Renewal 114

Worksheets 115

Sources 155

Index 157

ACKNOWLEDGMENTS

The TURBO FAST system was used to produce all computer spreadsheets in this manual. TURBO FAST is produced by Financial Proformas, Inc., 1855 Olympic Boulevard, Suite 200, Walnut Creek, California 94596.

PREFACE

Commercial Loan Analysis is a handbook for credit analysts, commercial lenders, and students of commercial lending. It is both a training manual for new analysts and an essential desk reference for experienced bankers. It focuses on financial and cash flow analysis, which is typically performed by credit analysts.

The book consists of step-by-step explanations of the basic aspects of commercial loan analysis, plus case studies for practical applications. Although it can be used easily by an analyst on his or her first day on the job, it is most effective in support of on-the-job training and real-life analysis. Its best use is as a reference guide while analyzing actual commercial borrowers.

The book only assumes existing, basic knowledge of the business world. Familiarity with basic financial/accounting tools and principles such as financial statements, interest calculations, business forms, and SWOT analysis is assumed. However, very little specific banking industry knowledge is necessary.

Chapter 1

INTRODUCTION TO COMMERCIAL LOAN ANALYSIS: A CRUCIAL BANK FUNCTION

COMMERCIAL LOAN ANALYSIS

Commercial loan analysis is a crucial bank function. Proper analysis helps minimize loan losses by identifying weaknesses in either prospective or existing loan relationships. In addition, analysis helps identify areas of strength as well as degree of risk. It can, therefore, be used not only to support loan approval decisions, but to support risk rating and pricing decisions.

Analysis (especially that of the bank's larger loan relationships) is typically performed by "Credit Analysts" who are members of a "Credit Department." The Credit Department should operate independently from the commercial lending function. Independence is necessary to ensure that loans are analyzed objectively and in a uniform manner.

Chapter 1

The loan analyst gathers information, analyzes it, and reports his or her findings to a loan officer or to a loan committee. Accuracy and objectivity are important because the loan officer or the committee makes decisions based upon the analysis. It is equally important for lenders to understand loan analysis since they make the final loan decision.

In addition to providing information for loan decisions, the analysis function provides the analyst with excellent experience and training for a career in commercial lending.

CASE STUDY

The following scenario and loan information is used throughout the book to illustrate various analytical techniques. The case study reflects a fairly typical bank lending relationship, and it includes both commercial and individual loans which will be evaluated.

Charlie's Chocolate Company, Incorporated is a manufacturer and wholesaler of fine chocolates and other chocolate products. The company's chocolates are sold primarily to candy stores and gift shops throughout the Midwest.

Mr. Charles Smith started the company in late 1990 by purchasing the equipment of a failing chocolate manufacturer. The company was incorporated as an Illinois Subchapter S corporation at that time.

Mr. Smith owns 100 percent of the common stock of the company. He has also made a $75,000 loan to the company. Currently, the company pays interest each month on this loan from Mr. Smith at an annual rate of 10.0 percent. The principal on the loan is not currently being repaid, and the loan is subordinate to all other debt per an agreement with the bank.

Mr. Smith also owns the building in which the company operates. He owns this building personally and rents it to the

Introduction to Commercial Loan Analysis

company. The company rents on a triple net basis; this means that the company (not Mr. Smith) pays for all taxes, insurance, and maintenance related to the building.

Mr. Smith and Charlie's Chocolate Company have a relationship at your bank consisting of the following seven loans:

1. A **$100,000** "short-term working capital" line of credit to the **company,** which is fully drawn at December 31, 1992. This line is renewed annually, and monthly payments of interest only are required. The interest rate is 8.0 percent.

2. A **$230,000** note to the **company** originally used to purchase the company's assets. Principal payments of $2,500 are required monthly along with accrued interest at 8.0 percent.

3. A **$58,000** note to the **company** which was made in 1993 to purchase additional equipment. The loan has 40 months' principal and interest amortization remaining. The interest rate is 8.0 percent, and the monthly fixed principal and interest payment is $1,657.

4. A **$500,000** commercial mortgage on the operating facility made to **Mr. Smith, personally**. Principal payments of $4,167 are required monthly along with accrued interest at 8.0 percent.

5. A **$50,000** commercial mortgage on a rental property made to **Mr. Smith**. Principal payments of $833 are required monthly along with accrued interest at 8.0 percent.

6. A **$5,000** auto loan made to **Mr. Smith**. The loan has two years' principal and interest amortization remaining.

Chapter 1

>The interest rate is 8.0 percent, and the monthly fixed principal and interest payment is $226.

7. A **$100,000** residential mortgage on **Mr. Smith's** home. The loan has 20 years, principal and interest amortization remaining. The interest rate is 8.0 percent, and the monthly fixed principal and interest payment is $836.

Although lending relationships can be quite complicated, analytical techniques allow the crucial issues to be highlighted so that accurate loan approval and risk rating decisions can be made.

Chapter 2

SPREADING AND ANALYZING FINANCIAL STATEMENTS

SPREADING

"Spreading" is the act of putting financial data supplied by a commercial loan customer or prospect into a computer via a "spreadsheet" program. Popular spreadsheet programs include TURBO FAST (by Financial Proformas, Inc.) and FAMAS (by Crowe, Chizek and Company, Certified Public Accountants). The analyst only enters balance sheet and income statement data into the spreadsheet program. From this, the program produces a complete set of financial information including balance sheets, income statements, cash flow statements, reconciliations, and ratios.

Historical or projected financial statements can be prepared internally by the borrower or externally by an accountant. Historical financial statements prepared by a CPA will explain the level of examination the accountant has made in

Chapter 2

a letter preceding the statements. Types of CPA prepared, **historical** statements are described as follows:

1. Compiled statements are CPA prepared, but the accountant makes no opinion as to the accuracy of the statements.

2. Reviewed statements are examined for accuracy by the accountant, but the examination is significantly less in scope than an audit.

3. A **Qualified Audit** results when the accountant strictly examines the financial statements. Account balances including loans, deposits, receivables, payables, and inventory are audited. The auditor also gives an opinion on the ability of the firm to continue as a going-concern.

   The audit is considered "qualified" because there is some discrepancy or disagreement between the borrower's figures and the auditor's findings. Any such discrepancies will be listed in the letter preceding the statements.

4. An **Unqualified Audit** is also a strict examination as described above except that it has no discrepancies between the borrower's figures and the auditors findings.

ASSETS

When spreading the balance sheet, put the amount of each account into the corresponding or most closely corresponding account on the computer spreadsheet. There are, however, certain situations when the bank looks at accounts differently than the borrower and its accountants. These special situations are explained below.

A negative balance in the **cash** account should always be spread as an **overdraft** in the liability section. A negative cash balance is an overdraft or a form of borrowing (either directly from the bank or indirectly through float time). To be conser-

Spreading and Analyzing Financial Statements

vative, the negative cash balance is considered to be debt. One effect of this is that debt to worth is higher if negative cash is spread as additional debt rather than as a deduction from assets. (See Ratio section.)

Inventory types (for example, raw materials, work in process, and finished goods) should be detailed as such, if it is possible to obtain a breakdown. Look in the notes to the statements for a detailed schedule.

Prepaid expenses can be aggregated into one, single account to make spreading and analysis easier. In general, all prepaids should be classified as **long-term assets** even if the statements classify them as current assets. Such assets are rarely of value to the bank upon liquidation, so they are excluded as liquid assets. (Prepaid taxes can, however, be classified as **current assets** if the statements classify them as such.)

Prepaid interest should be detailed separately from prepaids, since prepaid interest (along with "accrued interest" or "interest payable") affects the cash interest paid account on the Cash Flow statement. Since many spreadsheet programs have no pre-paid interest account, any prepaid interest can be entered as a negative (contra) balance to the interest payable account on the liabilities side.

Employee advances and **notes due from officers** should always be classified as **long-term assets** (regardless of how the statements classify them), as they are frequently uncollectible in the event of default or bankruptcy.

Franchise fees, **start-up costs, loan fees**, and **goodwill are all intangible assets** and should be spread as such since they have no real value. These assets are, therefore, excluded from tangible net worth calculations (See Ratio section).

Many banks also consider **officer or stockholder loans** and **leasehold improvements** to be **intangible assets**. Officer receivables are difficult to collect, so bank asset or debt to worth calculations typically exclude them as assets. Leasehold improvements usually hold no value to the bank when leased property is vacated so they are typically excluded as well.

LIABILITIES

Current/non-current liabilities should be classified correctly. Current liabilities are those which come due within a year; non-current liabilities are due in more than a year.

If any long-term debt exists, be sure to classify the **current portion of long-term debt (CPLTD)** in the current liabilities section. The current portion of long-term debt is the total **principal** portion of long-term debt due in the next year. If the statements provided do not detail the current portion of long-term debt, it is appropriate to calculate the amount yourself.

Notes payable to officers or stockholders are a cause for investigation. You need to know: 1) if a repayment schedule exists (to determine debt service requirements and whether the debt is current or non-current), and 2) if the debt is subordinated to the bank's loans.

If the debt is subordinated, then spread it in the category **Subordinated Debt/Liability**. Subordinated debt is not included as debt in the senior debt to worth ratio, but rather it is treated as equity (see Ratio section).

It is important to classify **accrued interest** separately from any other accruals since it affects the cash interest expense line of the Cash Flow statement.

INCOME STATEMENT

The income statement begins with the revenue account. If revenues are detailed as separate products or services on the

Spreading and Analyzing Financial Statements

raw financial statements, then detail each product or service in separate revenue accounts in the spread.

In general, all **direct expenses** ("Cost of Sales" or "Cost of Goods Sold") should be aggregated into one category called Cost of Sales/Revenues. In addition, all **operating expenses** are aggregated into one category called General and Administrative (G and A) Expense or Operating Expense.

Certain expenses are, however, detailed **separately** from general operating expenses (or from Cost of Sales/Revenues). Examine the notes and schedules to uncover any such expenses not detailed in the income statements. The following are separated for monitoring or for cash flow analysis by a bank (See Cash Flow and Debt Service Coverage Analysis):

1. Officer's Compensation—The bank will want to monitor how much the principals take out of the business as salaries. Also, officer's compensation is occasionally added back to the cash available calculation for debt service coverage analysis.

2. Rent Expense—Rent is frequently paid from a corporation to the principals of the company. In this case, rent may be added back to cash available. (If rent expense is from Cost of Sales, then break it out under "Cost of Sales—Rent").

3. Depreciation/Amortization—These are non-cash expenses. They are added back when calculating cash flows. (If from Cost of Sales, then break out under "Cost of Sales-Depreciation.")

4. Interest expense—This is detailed since it affects debt service coverage analysis.

5. Bad debt expense—This is monitored and analyzed by the bank, especially if receivables are taken as collateral.

Chapter 2

6. Income tax expense—This is monitored and analyzed by the bank. Note that payroll, real estate, and all other non-income taxes can be spread as general operating expenses.

7. Pension plan contributions and charitable contributions—These should be separated because they are discretionary and may, therefore, be added back to cash available.

In addition to the above operating expenses, all **non-operating expenses/income** are detailed individually. Such expense items include **extraordinary gains and losses, other income or expenses, interest income, and gains or losses on the disposition of assets**. These items do not reflect the regular and ongoing operations of the business. In fact, cash available calculations are adjusted by extraordinary gains/losses and gains/losses on asset sales because these represent non-operating activities.

Note, however, that in certain cases, gains or losses on asset sales may be a regular part of business operation. An example is a rental company that carries some of its rental inventory on the books as fixed assets. The selling of these assets does constitute part of the regular operations of the business. In this case, therefore, spread the resulting gains or losses as **operating expenses** or as **operating income or revenues**.

ANALYSIS OF SPREADS

There are many areas to examine when the spreads of financial statements have been completed.

Watch for **trends** in net profits, profit margins, sales, ratios, etc. Explore **why** these occur. For example, are sales increases comprised primarily of increased unit sales or in-

Spreading and Analyzing Financial Statements

creased prices? Have sales increases resulted from a better economy or from better marketing?

Compare the company's data to **industry averages** (using, for example, Robert Morris Associates' *Annual Statement Studies*[1]). What are the differences between the firm and the average firm in the Industry? What are the differences between the local economy and the U.S. economy?

Watch for **jumps** in liabilities such as long-term debt or in expenses on the income statement. Ask why, for example, bank debt jumped. Did this debt finance equipment purchases which will increase productivity or allow greater sales? Ask why, for example, sales salaries jumped. Did the company employ more salespeople; did these salespeople generate more sales for the year?

Watch for **unexplained adjustments to retained earnings**. These occur when, for example, the owners of the company have taken distributions from retained earnings and not reported the transaction on the financial statements. If you find a note in the financial statements, or if you are informed that the stockholders made a withdrawal or declared a dividend, then this is no cause for alarm. There are accounts in

---

[1] RMA cautions that the Statement Studies data be regarded only as a general guideline and not as an absolute industry norm. This is due to limited samples within categories, the categorization of companies by their primary Standard Industrial Classification (SIC) number only, and different methods of operation by companies within the same industry.

The 1992 Annual Statement Studies publication contains data on 392 lines of business. Send (or call) for ordering information:

Customer Service Department
Robert Morris Assoicates
P.O. Box 8500 S1140
Philadelphia, PA 19178
(215) 851-0585, Ext. 6

Chapter 2

spreadsheet programs for distributions; they follow the income statement data.

Unexplained adjustments become a problem if the borrower cannot explain why or how the adjustments were made. (Since stockholder withdrawals are generally deducted from cash available to service debt, it is important to find if unexplained adjustments are, indeed, withdrawals.)

Matching of assets and liabilities on a company's balance sheet is very important. The bank would like to see that long-term assets such as buildings, equipment, etc. are financed by long-term debt. For example, an asset with a useful life of 10 years should be financed by a term loan with an amortization of no more than 10 years. A short-term asset such as accounts receivable or inventory should be financed by short-term borrowing, such as a line of credit.

Accounts receivable, inventory, and accounts payable are components of working capital (short-term assets minus short-term liabilities). It is for the support of these that a firm will have a "short-term working capital line of credit." Such a line may be necessary to fund seasonal increases in inventory or to pay accounts payable until receivables flow in following heavy revenues. At the end of the busy period; however, a company should be able to pay off the line of credit and not be dependent upon it for long-term funds.

Capital requirements of a firm should be examined. Firms such as manufacturers will typically have large capital requirements for machinery and other assets. Such businesses are inherently more risky than service firms such as accounting or law firms, which require relatively fewer assets to do business.

Further, capital requirements will be considered when analyzing debt repayment ability. Firms which are required to frequently replace fixed assets have additional financing requirements. When the useful lives of the assets end, the firm

Spreading and Analyzing Financial Statements

will either have to replace the assets through its own cash flow (a drain on cash available) or borrow (additional debt service) or both. (See Analysis of Capital Expenditures in the Cash Flow section).

CASE STUDY: CHARLIE'S CHOCOLATE COMPANY

Mr. Smith's accountant has just completed the fiscal year-end financial statements dated December 31, 1993 for Charlie's Chocolate Company, Inc. In addition to providing the statements, the accountant informs the bank that Charlie's Chocolate Company paid Mr. Smith a $10,000 dividend in 1993. This dividend is not listed anywhere on the financial statements. These statements comprise Exhibits 2.1 to 2.5.

Chapter 2

Exhibit 2.1

RYAN JONES
CERTIFIED PUBLIC ACCOUNTANT

**Board of Directors
Charlie's Chocolate Company, Inc.**

We have compiled the accompanying balance sheet as of December 31, 1993 and related statements of operations for the period January 1, 1993 through December 31, 1993, in accordance with standards established by the American Institute of Certified Public Accountants.

A compilation is limited to presenting, in the form of financial statements, information that is the representation of management. We have not audited or reviewed the accompanying financial statements, and, accordingly, do not express an opinion or other form of assurance on them.

Substantially all of the disclosures and the statement of cash flows required by generally accepted accounting principles are omitted from these statements. If the omitted disclosures and statements of cash flows were included in the financial statements, they might influence the user's conclusions about the company's financial position, results of operations, and cash flows. Accordingly, these financial statements are not designed for those who are not informed about such matters.

Spreading and Analyzing Financial Statements

Exhibit 2.2
Charlie's Chocolate Company, Inc.
Balance Sheet
December 31, 1993

Assets
  Current Assets

Cash	(41,000)	
Accounts Receivable	277,000	
Inventory (See Schedule)	298,000	
Prepaid Expenses	39,000	
Due From Employee	12,000	
Total Current Assets		585,000

  Fixed Assets

Mixing Equipment	110,000	
Accumulated Depreciation—Mixing	(70,000)	
Packaging	170,000	
Accumulated Depreciation—Packaging	(90,000)	
Vehicles	15,000	
Accumulated Depreciation—Vehicles	(4,000)	
Total Fixed Assets		131,000

  Other Assets

Goodwill (Net of Amortization)	15,000	
Total Other Assets		<u>15,000</u>

  Total Assets   731,000

See Accompanying Accountant's Report

Chapter 2

Exhibit 2.3
Charlie's Chocolate Company, Inc.
Balance Sheet
December 31, 1993

Liabilities
  Current Liabilities

Line of Credit—Bank	100,000	
Current Portion of Long-Term Debt	40,000	
Accounts Payable	103,000	
Accrued Salaries	19,000	
Accrued Interest	3,000	
Total Current Liabilities		265,000

  Long-Term Liabilities

Note Payable—Bank	230,000	
Note Payable—Bank	58,000	
Note Payable—Officer	75,000	
Total Long-Term Liabilities		363,000
Total Liabilities		628,000

Capital

Capital Stock	1,000	
Additional Paid in Capital	99,000	
Retained Earnings	3,000	
Total Capital		103,000
Total Liabilities and Capital		731,000

See Accompanying Accountant's Report

Spreading and Analyzing Financial Statements

Exhibit 2.4
Charlie's Chocolate Company, Inc.
Income Sheet
Twelve Months Ended December 31, 1993

Sales		1,290,000
Cost of Sales (See Schedule)		<u>684,000</u>
Gross Profit		606,000
Expenses (See Schedule)		572,000
Other (Income) / Expenses		
Interest Expense	36,000	
Gain on Sale of Assets	(12,000)	
Total Other (Income) / Expense		<u>24,000</u>
Net Income		10,000

See Accompanying Accountant's Report

Chapter 2

Exhibit 2.5
Charlie's Chocolate Company, Inc.
Expense Breakdown
Twelve Months Ended December 31, 1993

Inventory	
Cocoa	90,000
Sugar	136,000
Other Ingredients	40,000
Finished Chocolate	<u>32,000</u>
Total Inventory	298,000
Cost of Goods Sold	
Beginning Inventory	197,000
Purchases	283,000
Ending Inventory	(298,000)
Production Costs	323,000
Direct Labor	149,000
Depreciation	<u>30,000</u>
Total Cost of Sales	684,000
Expenses	
Salaries	179,000
Officer's Salary	105,000
Employee Benefits	38,000
Payroll tax	31,000
Rent	110,000
Insurance	3,000
Utilities	6,000
Real estate tax	15,000
License & fees	2,000
Repairs	7,000
Postage	1,000
Promotional	16,000
Office Supplies	3,000
Uncollectible Debts	16,000
Depreciation	25,000
Amortization	5,000
Contribution to charity	<u>10,000</u>
Total Expenses	572,000

See Accompanying Accountant's Report

Spreading and Analyzing Financial Statements

SPREADING THE FINANCIAL STATEMENTS

Balance Sheet—Assets

First, note the level of examination that the accountant has made. The accountant states in the letter preceding the financials that the statements have been **compiled**. This means that the accountant has not examined the statements for accuracy. He has merely taken financial data supplied by Charlie's Chocolate Company and put it into the format of a balance sheet and an income statement. Compiled statements are only as reliable as the company's numbers.

The first account to spread is the cash account. Notice that this account has a negative balance. This is actually a form of borrowing and should be spread as an overdraft in the current liability section. **Enter $41,000 in the Overdraft account**. (Note that this action will add $41,000 to both the total assets and the total liabilities and net worth. This total will now be $772,000)

Next, **enter $277,000 in the Accounts Receivable—Trade Account**.

The inventory line on the balance sheet refers to a schedule. Since inventory should be categorized when possible, this schedule should be examined. **Enter the total raw materials inventory of $266,000. Enter the total finished goods inventory of $32,000.**

Prepaid expenses are next. Even though the accountant considers prepaids to be current assets, the bank considers prepaids to be non-current assets. **Enter $39,000 in Prepaids—Non Current**.

The next account represents a loan due from an employee. The bank considers employee, officer, and stockholder loans to be non-current assets. **Enter $12,000 in Non-Current Accounts or Notes Receivable**.

19

Chapter 2

Fixed assets are listed next. It is helpful to detail land, buildings, leasehold improvements, machinery and equipment, furniture and fixtures, and transportation equipment. However, it is not necessary to detail assets within these categories. It appears that "Mixing Equipment" and "Packaging" both fall under the category of Machinery and Equipment. **Enter $280,000 in Machinery and Equipment. Enter $15,000 in Vehicles.** It is not usually necessary to detail depreciation separately for each asset. **Enter $164,000 in Accumulated Depreciation**.

Enter $15,000 in the Goodwill account in the Intangible Assets section.

Balance Sheet—Liabilities

Lines of credit represent short-term borrowing. **Enter $100,000 in Notes Payable Short Term—Bank.**

Whenever long-term debt on a regular repayment plan exists, the principal amount to be repaid in the next year should be spread as current portion of long-term debt. (If the accountant had not detailed this, it would have been appropriate to calculate the amount manually and to have separated it from long-term debt.) **Enter $40,000 in Current Portion of Long-Term Debt**.

Enter $103,000 in the Accounts Payable—Trade account.

Enter $19,000 in the Wages/Salaries Payable account. **Enter $3,000 in the Interest Payable account**. Note that these should be detailed separately and that accrued expenses are current liabilities.

Enter $288,000 in Total Long-Term Debt. Generally, long-term debts do not need to be detailed separately.

Since the officer debt is subordinated and it is not currently being repaid, **enter $75,000 in Subordinated Debt Liability—Officer/Stockholder**.

Spreading and Analyzing Financial Statements

Enter $1,000 in Common Stock, $99,000 in Paid in Capital, and $3,000 in Retained Earnings.

Income Statement

Enter $1,290,000 in Sales/Revenues.

In general, each expense comprising the total cost of sales does not need to be detailed; however, depreciation or rent in cost of sales should be detailed separately. Since a schedule is provided, it should be examined to look for such expenses. Since the schedule details $30,000 of depreciation expense in cost of goods sold, **enter $654,000 in Cost of Goods Sold. Enter $30,000 in Cost of Goods Sold-Depreciation.**

Examine the schedule of expenses, and detail the following **separately as operating expenses**:

1. Officer's Salary:		$105,000
2. Rent:		$110,000
3. Bad Debt Expense:		$ 16,000
4. Depreciation:		$ 25,000
5. Amortization:		$ 5,000

Enter the $10,000 of Charitable Contributions in Other Expenses.

Enter the remaining total, $301,000 (from the accountant's total expenses of $572,000), as General and Administrative Expense.

Enter $36,000 in the Interest Expense account.

Enter $12,000 in the Gain on Sale of Assets Account.

A dividend payment was mentioned by the accountant. Although this payment does not appear in the financial statements, it is an important transaction to consider. **Enter**

Chapter 2

$10,000 in the dividends paid account after the income statement information.

The completed spreadsheets including ratios for fiscal year-ends December 31, 1991, December 31, 1992, and December 31, 1993 follow (See Exhibits 2.6 to 2.10). The TURBO FAST system by Financial Proformas, Inc. has been used to spread the financial statements.

ANALYZING THE COMPLETED SPREADS

When the spread is completed, examine the equity section of the balance sheet. The retained earnings balance remained at $3,000 in 1993 despite the fact that the company made $10,000 during the year. If the $10,000 dividend had not been mentioned by the accountant and entered in the spread, the spreadsheet program would have alerted the user of an unexplained adjustment to retained earnings. That is, the retained earnings change from December 31, 1992 to December 31, 1993 would not have reconciled with net income for 1993.

In addition to the retained earnings reconciliation, a wealth of information is supplied by the spread. The analysis process begins by examination of this spread. First, note any trends or sudden changes that strike you.

The most striking trend is the overall growth of the company from 1990 to 1993. The company has shown rapid growth when measured by total assets, and, more importantly, when measured by sales. Explore **why** this growth occurred. Perhaps unit sales have remained constant, while prices have increased. Perhaps unit sales have soared because of a superior chocolate bar. The growth trend will be an important factor when analyzing ratios and debt service coverage in later chapters.

Note that long-term debt increased during 1993. It is important to explore **why** debt increased as well as **what it**

Spreading and Analyzing Financial Statements

Exhibit 2.6

```
                          CHARLIE'S CHOCOLATE COMPANY, INC.
FAST 4.3                        Common Size Report                     02/25/94
General Industries                                                     11:57 A.M.

SIC Code : 2064_
Auditor : Ryan Jones, CPA          CPA PRP        CPA PRP        CPA PRP
Analyst : Ken Pirok                Dec 31         Dec 31         Dec 31
                                    1991           1992           1993
AMOUNTS IN THOUSANDS OF DOLLARS    12 Mth         12 Mth         12 Mth
================================================================================
COMMON SIZE REPORT                   $     %        $     %        $     %
================================================================================
ASSETS:
--------------------------------------------------------------------------------
Cash                                 44    8.1      28    5.0    .......  .......

   Accounts Receivable - Trade      95   17.6     151   26.8     277   35.9

   Raw Materials                   135   25.0     172   30.5     266   34.5
   Finished Goods                   30    5.6      25    4.4      32    4.1
                                   ---------------------------------------------
Total Inventory                    165   30.6     197   34.9     298   38.6
                                   ---------------------------------------------
   TOTAL CURRENT ASSETS            304   56.3     376   66.7     575   74.5

   Machinery & Equipment           228   42.2     228   40.4     280   36.3
   Transportation Equipment         15    2.8      15    2.7      15    1.9
                                   ---------------------------------------------
Gross Fixed Assets                 243   45.0     243   43.1     295   38.2
   less: Accumulated Depreciation   59   10.9     109   19.3     164   21.2
                                   ---------------------------------------------
Total Fixed Assets - Net           184   34.1     134   23.8     131   17.0

Due from Employees               .......  .......  .......  .......   12    1.6

Prepaid Expenses - Non Current      27    5.0      34    6.0      39    5.1

   INTANGIBLES
   Goodwill - Net                   25    4.6      20    3.5      15    1.9
                                   ---------------------------------------------
NON-CURRENT ASSETS                 236   43.7     188   33.3     197   25.5
                                   ---------------------------------------------
   TOTAL ASSETS                    540  100.0     564  100.0     772  100.0
================================================================================
```

23

Chapter 2

Exhibit 2.7

```
                              CHARLIE'S CHOCOLATE COMPANY, INC.
FAST 4.3                           Common Size Report                        02/25/94
General Industries                                                           11:57 A.M.

SIC Code : 2064_
Auditor : Ryan Jones, CPA      CPA PRP           CPA PRP           CPA PRP
Analyst : Ken Pirok            Dec 31            Dec 31            Dec 31
                               1991              1992              1993
AMOUNTS IN THOUSANDS OF DOLLARS 12 Mth           12 Mth            12 Mth
```

LIABILITIES	$	%	$	%	$	%
Overdraft	......	......	......	......	41	5.3
Notes Payable S/T - Bank	5	0.9	36	6.4	100	13.0
Current Maturities LTD	30	5.6	30	5.3	40	5.2
Accounts Payable - Trade	50	9.3	45	8.0	103	13.3
Wages/Salaries Payable	5	0.9	15	2.7	19	2.5
Interest Payable	......	......	......	......	3	0.4
Total Accrued Liabilities	5	0.9	15	2.7	22	2.8
TOTAL CURRENT LIABILITIES	90	16.7	126	22.3	306	39.6
Exist Long Term Debt	290	53.7	260	46.1	288	37.3
TOTAL SENIOR LT LIABILITIES	290	53.7	260	46.1	288	37.3
TOTAL SENIOR LIABILITIES	380	70.4	386	68.4	594	76.9
Subordinated Debt	75	13.9	75	13.3	75	9.7
TOTAL LIABILITIES	455	84.3	461	81.7	669	86.7
NET WORTH						
Common Stock	1	0.2	1	0.2	1	0.1
Paid In Capital	99	18.3	99	17.6	99	12.8
Retained Earnings	-15	-2.8	3	0.5	3	0.4
NET WORTH	85	15.7	103	18.3	103	13.3
TOTAL LIABILITIES & NET WORTH	540	100.0	564	100.0	772	100.0
Tangible Net Worth	60	11.1	83	14.7	88	11.4
Working Capital	214	39.6	250	44.3	269	34.8

Spreading and Analyzing Financial Statements

Exhibit 2.8

```
                            CHARLIE'S CHOCOLATE COMPANY, INC.
FAST 4.3                         Common Size Report                        02/25/94
General Industries                                                         11:57 A.M.

SIC Code : 2064_
Auditor : Ryan Jones, CPA        CPA PRP          CPA PRP          CPA PRP
Analyst : Ken Pirok              Dec 31           Dec 31           Dec 31
                                  1991             1992             1993
AMOUNTS IN THOUSANDS OF DOLLARS  12 Mth           12 Mth           12 Mth
=====================================================================================
   I N C O M E   S T A T E M E N T     $      %       $      %       $      %
-------------------------------------------------------------------------------------
   Sales (Product 1)                  795  100.0    957  100.0   1,290  100.0

Cost of Goods Sold (Product 1)        400   50.3    458   47.9     654   50.7
Depreciation in CoGS                   25    3.1     25    2.6      30    2.3
                                      ---------    ---------     ---------
   GROSS PROFIT/REVENUES              370   46.5    474   49.5     606   47.0
                                      ---------    ---------     ---------

General & Administrative Expense      230   28.9    244   25.5     301   23.3
Officers Compensation                  30    3.8     50    5.2     105    8.1
Lease & Rental Expense                100   12.6    100   10.4     110    8.5
Bad Debt Expense                    ......  .....  ......  ....     16    1.2
Depreciation                           10    1.3     25    2.6      25    1.9
Amortization                            5    0.6      5    0.5       5    0.4
                                      ---------    ---------     ---------
   TOTAL OPERATING EXPENSES           375   47.2    424   44.3     562   43.6
                                      ---------    ---------     ---------
   OPERATING INCOME                    -5   -0.6     50    5.2      44    3.4

Interest Expense                       21    2.6     27    2.8      36    2.8
                                      ---------    ---------     ---------
   TOTAL INTEREST EXPENSE              21    2.6     27    2.8      36    2.8

Gain on Sale of Assets              ......  .....  ......  ....     12    0.9
Charitable Contributions            ......  .....  ......  ....     10    0.8
                                      ---------    ---------     ---------
   NET PROFIT                         -26   -3.3     23    2.4      10    0.8

Cash Dividend - Common Stock        ......  .....      5    0.5     10    0.8
                                      ---------    ---------     ---------
   CHANGE IN NET WORTH                -26   -3.3     18    1.9   ......  .....
=====================================================================================
```

Chapter 2

Exhibit 2.9

```
                    CHARLIE'S CHOCOLATE COMPANY, INC.
         FAST 4.3            Cash Flow              02/25/94
         General Industries                         11:57 A.M.

         SIC Code : 2064_
         Auditor : Ryan Jones, CPA           CPA PRP  CPA PRP
         Analyst : Ken Pirok                 Dec 31   Dec 31
                                              1992     1993
         AMOUNTS IN THOUSANDS OF DOLLARS    12 Mth   12 Mth
         ======================================================
         C A S H F L O W
         ------------------------------------------------------
         Sales - Net                            957    1,290
         Change in Receivables                  -56     -126
                                              --------------
         CASH FROM SALES                        901    1,164

         Cost of Goods Sold                    -458     -654
         Change in Inventories                  -32     -101
         Change in Payables                      -5       58
                                              --------------
         CASH PRODUCTION COSTS                 -495     -697
                                              --------------
         GROSS CASH PROFITS                     406      467

         SG & A Expense                        -394     -532
         Change in Prepaids                      -7       -5
         Change in Accruals                      10        4
                                              --------------
         Cash Operating Expense                -391     -533
                                              --------------
         CASH AFTER OPERATIONS                   15      -66

         Miscellaneous Cash Income           .......    -22
                                              --------------
         NET CASH AFTER OPERATIONS               15      -88

         Interest Expense                       -27      -33
         Dividends Paid                          -5      -10
                                              --------------
         Financing Costs                        -32      -43

         NET CASH INCOME                        -17     -131

         Current Portion Long Term Debt         -30      -30
                                              --------------
         CASH AFTER DEBT AMORTIZATION           -47     -161

         Capital Expenditures - Tangible     .......    -40
                                              --------------
         FINANCING SURPLUS/(REQUIREMENTS)       -47     -201

         Change in Short Term Debt               31      105
         Change in Long Term Debt            .......     68
                                              --------------
         Total External Financing                31      173
                                              --------------
         Cash After Financing                   -16      -28
         Actual Change in Cash                  -16      -28
         ======================================================
         Net Income + Depreciation               78       70

         Misc Cash Income Detail:
         Other Non-Current Assets            .......    -12
         Other Expense                       .......    -10
                                              --------------
         Total                               .......    -22
         ======================================================
```

Spreading and Analyzing Financial Statements

Exhibit 2.10

```
                    CHARLIE'S CHOCOLATE COMPANY, INC.
FAST 4.3              Financial Ratios              02/25/94
General Industries                                  11:57 A.M.

SIC Code : 2064_
Auditor : Ryan Jones, CPA          CPA PRP CPA PRP CPA PRP
Analyst : Ken Pirok                Dec 31  Dec 31  Dec 31
                                    1991    1992    1993
AMOUNTS IN THOUSANDS OF DOLLARS    12 Mth  12 Mth  12 Mth
=============================================================
F I N A N C I A L   R A T I O S
-------------------------------------------------------------
GROWTH RATIOS:
Net Sales Growth, Composite %        N/A    20.38   34.80
   Sales Growth, Sales (Product 1)   N/A    20.38   34.80
Net Income Growth, %                 N/A   188.46  -56.52
Total Assets Growth, %               N/A     4.44   36.88
Total Liabilities Growth, %          N/A     1.32   45.12
Net Worth Growth, %                  N/A    21.18   .......
-------------------------------------------------------------
PROFITABILITY RATIOS:
Gross Margin, Composite %          49.69   52.14   49.30
   Margin, Sales (Product 1)      49.69   52.14   49.30
SG & A, %                          45.28   41.17   41.24
Cushion (Gross Margin - SG & A), %  4.40   10.97    8.06
Depreciation, Amortization, %       5.03    5.75    4.65
Operating Profit Margin, %         -0.63    5.22    3.41
Interest Expense, %                 2.64    2.82    2.79
Operating Margin, %                -3.27    2.40    0.62
Net Margin, %                      -3.27    2.40    0.78
Return on Average Assets, %          N/A    4.17    1.50
Return on Average Equity, %          N/A   32.17   11.70
Dividend Payout Rate, %          .......   21.74  100.00
-------------------------------------------------------------
COVERAGE RATIOS:
EBITDA / (Total Interest + CMLTD)    N/A    1.84    1.61
Interest Coverage (EBIT / Interest) -0.24   1.85    1.28
Net Income + Depreciation / CMLTD    N/A    2.60    2.33
-------------------------------------------------------------
ACTIVITY RATIOS:
Receivables in Days                   44      58      78
Inventory in Days                    151     157     166
Payables in Days                      46      36      57
Total Assets / Net sales            0.68    0.59    0.60
-------------------------------------------------------------
LIQUIDITY RATIOS:
Working Capital                      214     250     269
Quick Ratio                         1.54    1.42    0.91
Current Ratio                       3.38    2.98    1.88
Sales / Net Working Capital         3.71    3.83    4.80
-------------------------------------------------------------
LEVERAGE RATIOS:
Total Liabilities / T Net Worth     7.58    5.55    7.60
Tot Sr. Liabs. / TNW & Sub Debt     2.81    2.44    3.64
Borrowed Funds / TNW & Sub Debt     2.41    2.06    2.88
Long-Term Debt / Net Fixed Assets   1.74    2.16    2.50
-------------------------------------------------------------
CASH POSITION:
Cash Margin               %          N/A   42.42   36.20
Cash Coverage                        N/A    0.24   -1.21
Net Cash Income                      N/A     -17    -131
Net Income + Depreciation             14      78      70
-------------------------------------------------------------
SUSTAINABLE GROWTH & BANKRUPTCY:
Sustainable Growth, (N/(T-N))  %     N/A   12.34  .......
Z=1.2x1 +1.4x2 +3.3x3 +.6x4 +.999x5 1.99    2.66    2.38
=============================================================
```

Chapter 2

finances. You learn that a loan was made to finance the purchase of additional equipment. You also learn that the loan is amortized over four years, which is roughly the useful life of the equipment. The loan's amortization does, indeed, match the expected life of the asset.

A further question to ask is, specifically, what equipment was purchased. You learn that the equipment is used to manufacture white chocolate, an item which has become popular for competing chocolate manufacturers. According to Mr. Smith, the addition of this product will lead to new white chocolate sales and solidify the company's position of supplying all chocolate needs.

Chapter 3

RATIO ANALYSIS

Comparing the values of various financial accounts to form ratios provides a useful tool to analyze financial structure and operations. Numerous financial ratios exist; some of the most common are presented here. Actual ratios from the case study are examined afterwards.

LIQUIDITY RATIOS

"Liquidity" or "current position" is measured by ability to service short-term debt (or "current" liabilities) through "liquidation" of current assets. Short-term debt consists of any obligations due in one year or less. This includes overdrafts, short-term accounts and notes payable, current maturities of long-term debt, and accrued liabilities. Current assets are comprised of cash, cash equivalents (such as time deposits or marketable securities), accounts receivable, and inventory.

Chapter 3

Current Ratio[2] = total current assets/total current liabilities

The current ratio measures ability to service current liabilities through the "liquidation" of current assets. The higher the ratio, the greater the liquidity since there is a larger "cushion" between current assets and current liabilities.

It is also important to analyze the composition and quality of current assets. For example, are current assets comprised primarily of cash and liquid assets, or are they comprised of receivables which may be difficult to collect? If current assets are comprised primarily of cash and cash equivalents, then the company is considered to be more liquid than if current assets are comprised primarily of receivables and/or inventory.

$$\text{Quick Ratio or Acid Test}[2] = \frac{\text{(cash \& equivalents + accounts / notes receivable)}}{\text{total current liabilities}}$$

The quick ratio is a more conservative measure of liquidity since the numerator includes only the most liquid assets and excludes inventory. In general, if the quick ratio is less than one-to-one, this implies that the company will be dependent upon the liquidation of inventory to service short-term debts.

Working Capital = total current assets − total current liabilities

The interpretation of working capital is similar to that of the current ratio except that the cushion between current

---

[2] Robert Morris Associates. Annual Statement Studies. Copyright 1992 by Robert Morris Associates. Reprinted with permission from Annual Statement Studies, 1992. pp. 10–15.

Ratio Analysis

assets and current liabilities is measured as the dollar amount difference.

TURNOVER/ACTIVITY RATIOS

Activity ratios measure "turnover" or the rate at which receivables, inventory, and payables are created and then used up or paid off through operations. Quicker turnover ratios generally imply greater efficiency and better management of operations.

$$\text{Receivables Turnover Ratio }[2] = \frac{\text{net revenue}}{\text{trade accounts and notes receivable}}$$

Receivables turnover represents the average number of times per year that trade receivables "turn over" or are converted to cash. A higher (more rapid) turnover is more favorable since sales on credit are converted to cash more quickly. A lower (less rapid) turnover is unfavorable since default becomes more likely as receivables remain uncollected.

A problem with this ratio is that it measures receivables at one point-in-time against an entire period (usually a year) of sales. The measurement does not, therefore, consider seasonal fluctuations in sales.

Another problem with this ratio exists when cash sales represent a large percentage of net revenue; the ratio will be very favorable in this case. A more accurate measure can be taken by constructing a ratio considering only credit sales in the numerator.

$$\text{Receivables Days }[2] = \frac{365}{\text{receivables turnover ratio}}$$

Receivables days expresses turnover as the average length of time in days between a sale and the cash collection

Chapter 3

of the receivable. A lower value (more rapid turnover) is more favorable. Interpretation and problems are similar to those of the receivables turnover ratio: seasonal fluctuations are averaged out, and if net revenue is largely comprised of cash sales, then receivable collection is diminished.

Inventory Turnover Ratio[2] = cost of sales/inventory

Inventory turnover represents the average number of times per year that inventory "turns over" or that goods are sold from inventory. A higher (more rapid) turnover is generally more favorable since goods are being sold more quickly. Rapid turnover can, however, be a symptom of inventory shortage.

A lower (less rapid) turnover can indicate poor liquidity, overstocking, or obsolescence. Slow inventory turnover can also result from planned seasonal build-ups.

This ratio compares inventory at a point-in-time to an entire period's costs of sales. The ratio is, therefore, affected by seasonal fluctuations in inventory.

Inventory Days[2] = $\dfrac{365}{\text{receivables turnover ratio}}$

Inventory days expresses turnover as the average length of time in days between purchase and sale of inventory. A lower value (more rapid turnover) is generally more favorable. Interpretation and problems are similar to those of the inventory turnover ratio.

Payables Turnover Ratio[2] = $\dfrac{\text{cost of sales}}{\text{trade accounts \& notes receivable}}$

Ratio Analysis

Payables turnover represents the average number of times per year that trade accounts payable "turn over" or that inventory purchases on credit are paid for with cash. A higher (more rapid) turnover is generally more favorable since payables are being paid more quickly. However, paying trade debts too quickly can use up needed cash. A lower (less rapid) turnover can result from cash shortages or from disputed invoices or extended payment terms from suppliers.

A problem is that this ratio compares payables at a point-in-time to an entire period's costs of sales.

$$\textbf{Payables Days}^2 = \frac{365}{\text{cost of sales/payables turnover ratio}}$$

Payables days expresses turnover as the average time in days between purchases and their payment. Interpretation and problems are similar to those of the payables turnover ratio.

LEVERAGE RATIOS

"Leverage" is the measurement of the use of debt financing. Higher leverage implies a greater proportion of debt financing to equity financing. Higher risk generally accompanies higher leverage.

Debt/Worth^2 = total liabilities /net worth

The debt to worth ratio represents the relationship between capital contributed by creditors and that contributed by owners. For example, if debt to worth is 3.5 to 1, then for every $1.00 the owners have put in, they have borrowed $3.50 to operate. A higher ratio implies greater risk. A lower ratio implies safety or additional debt capacity.

Chapter 3

Heavily depreciated buildings can cause an artificially high debt to worth if the market values of the buildings are significantly higher than the book values. This occurs because, although the value of the buildings is relatively small on the books, the market value that they would bring if sold is significantly higher.

Total Senior Debt / Tangible Net Worth

The relationship between senior debt and tangible worth has an interpretation similar to that of the debt to worth ratio; however, it considers only **senior** debt against **tangible** net worth. Subordinated debt is excluded from the debt calculation and is, instead, treated as equity (or capital contributed by owners). Also, intangibles such as goodwill or agreements not-to-compete are subtracted from equity.

This ratio is useful when, for example, officer debt is subordinated to bank debt. In the event of liquidation, the senior bank debt would be repaid in full before subordinated officer debt. For this reason, the subordinated debt is treated as equity.

COVERAGE RATIOS

$$\text{EBIT/Interest Ratio} = \frac{\text{earnings before interest \& taxes}}{\text{annual interest expense}}$$

The EBIT/Interest Ratio measures interest expense coverage by profits. A higher ratio implies greater ability to service interest expense.

$$\frac{\text{Cash Flow}}{\text{CMLTD}} = \frac{\text{net profit} + \text{depreciation, amortization, depletion}}{\text{current portion maturities of long}-\text{term debt}}$$

Ratio Analysis

Cash Flow/CMLTD measures coverage of current maturities of long-term debt by accrual basis cash flow. See the chapter on cash flow analysis for a more detailed explanation of interpreting cash flows.

PROFITABILITY/EFFICIENCY/ OPERATING RATIOS

$$\text{Gross Profit Margin} = \frac{\text{net revenue} - \text{total cost of sales}}{\text{net revenue}}$$

The gross profit margin expresses gross profit (total sales less cost of sales) as a percentage of total sales.

$$\text{Operating Profit Margin} = \frac{\text{net revenue} - \text{cost of sales} - \text{operating expenses}}{\text{net revenue}}$$

Operating profit margin (also known as "Cushion") expresses the operating profit (sales, less cost of sales, less operating expenses) as a percentage of total sales.

Expense/Sales Ratios

Any expense can be expressed as a percentage of sales. It may be particularly useful to divide depreciation, officers' salaries, rents, or any particular expense by total sales and use the resulting ratio for comparison to historical data or to industry averages.

$$\text{Net Profit Margin} = \frac{\text{net income}}{\text{net revenue}}$$

Chapter 3

Net profit margin measures net income as a percentage of total sales. It is a good indicator of overall profitability, and it is a component of the return on assets (ROA) and the return on equity (ROE) ratios.

Sales/Total Assets[2] = net revenue / total assets

Sales/Total assets represents ability to generate revenues based on total assets. This ratio is useful when compared to other companies (using, for example, RMA averages) in the specific industry that you are analyzing. This ratio should also be analyzed along with the other efficiency ratios (such as net profit margin—see ROA) to get a complete measure of efficiency.

$$\textbf{Return on Assets (ROA)} = \frac{\text{net income}}{\text{net revenue}} \times \frac{\text{net revenue}}{\text{total assets}} = \frac{\text{net income}}{\text{total assets}}$$

ROA measures return on total assets. Heavily depreciated assets or the presence of a large proportion of intangible assets can distort this ratio.

It is important to note the inverse relationship between the two ratios comprising return on assets. All things being equal, a firm whose sales/assets ratio is high (i.e., has a large dollar amount of sales from each dollar of assets employed in the business) will have lower profitability as measured by the net profit/sales ratio (or the "net profit margin"). The reason is that firms with smaller asset requirements need less borrowing and have shorter turnaround times. Therefore, such firms have less risk and, consequently, smaller returns.

$$\textbf{Return on Equity (ROE)} = \frac{\text{net income}}{\text{net revenue}} \times \frac{\text{net revenue}}{\text{total assets}} \times \frac{\text{total assets}}{\text{equity}} = \frac{\text{net income}}{\text{equity}}$$

Ratio Analysis

ROE measures return on total equity. Notice that equity is measured by the book value, which may differ from market value. Notice also that the ROE formula represents ROA multiplied by assets/equity. Assets divided by equity is a measure of leverage. Because of this, ROE indicates the effect of leverage on return.

Sales/Net Fixed Assets[2] = net revenue/net fixed assets

Sales/net fixed assets represents productivity of property, plant, and equipment as measured by the level of revenues. Note that productivity is also measured by, for example, **profit before taxes** or **cash flow**. Such values can be substituted into the numerator to create more productivity measurements. Note that heavily depreciated assets can distort such ratios.

Sales/Working Capital Ratio = net revenue/net working capital

Sales/working capital represents ability to generate sales based on working capital.

BREAKEVEN RATIOS

$$\frac{\text{Breakeven}}{\text{Revenue}} = \frac{\text{fixed expense} + \text{annual debt service}}{1 - \text{variable expense percentage of revenue}}$$

Breakeven revenue represents the dollar amount of revenues necessary to service all expense and debt requirements. This measurement is useful when used with debt service coverage ratios.

Fixed expense excludes non-cash expenses such as depreciation as well as interest expense. Annual debt service includes both principal and interest payments. Variable ex-

Chapter 3

pense percentage of revenue equals total variable expenses divided by total revenue.

When using the breakeven revenue formula for **real estate properties**, vacancy and bad debt expenses should be **excluded** as both fixed and variable expenses. Also, an additional calculation can be made for rental properties or hotels/motels:

$$\text{Breakeven Occupancy Percentage} = \frac{\text{breakeven revenue}}{\text{total revenue if fully occupied}}$$

Breakeven occupancy percentage represents the percentage of total units that must be rented so that debt service and expenses can be met.

A simpler expression of the breakeven revenue formula for **conventional commercial and industrial lending** is:

$$\text{Breakeven Revenue} = \frac{\text{fixed expense} + \text{annual debt service}}{\text{gross profit margin}}$$

Note that this breakeven revenue formula assumes that all costs of sales are variable in nature.

CASE STUDY: ANALYSIS OF CHARLIE'S CHOCOLATE COMPANY'S RATIOS

Charlie's Chocolate Company's ratios are calculated on the final page of the spreadsheet. The following analysis details the various signals and trends which are highlighted by financial ratios.

Ratio Analysis

LIQUIDITY RATIOS

Working capital appears adequate. As of December 31, 1993, there is a $269,000 cushion between current assets and current liabilities.

Although it has declined each year, the current ratio (total current assets divided by total current liabilities) also appears adequate.

The quick ratio measures cash, cash equivalents, and receivables divided by total current liabilities. By excluding inventory in the numerator, the quick ratio alerts the analyst to dependency on inventory turnover to service short-term liabilities. If this ratio falls below 1:1 (as it has at December 31, 1993), then the company may need to rely on increased inventory turnover to service short-term debt payments.

TURNOVER RATIOS

Receivables turnover slowed in both 1992 and 1993. This means that accounts receivable have been collected and converted into cash more and more slowly. The quality of these receivables should be analyzed. Are receivables primarily due from large retailers or from small "mom and pop" operations? Do the major customers who use credit have good reputations and strong financial conditions, or do they have histories of repayment problems?

Inventory turnover has remained above 150 days, and it is rising. Goods were held in inventory for an average of 166 days in 1993. What could be causing the slow inventory turnover?

Perhaps the company has been building up inventory in anticipation of increasing sales. If so, it appears that they have been consistently over-estimating their inventory needs.

Chapter 3

Perhaps the company has been taking advantage of lower sugar and cocoa prices by stocking up. This may or may not be appropriate since the food could spoil. The bank should ask the company why inventory turnover is so slow and how the inventory is stored.

Payables turnover improved in 1992 but slowed to 57 days in 1993. Perhaps suppliers now offer extended payment terms. Or, more likely, perhaps since cash was relatively short in 1993, the company extended its payables to provide needed cash. (See cash flow analysis.)

LEVERAGE RATIOS

Debt to worth (total liabilities divided by net worth) represents the relationship between capital contributed by creditors and capital contributed by owners. A higher ratio, especially above two or three to one, implies greater risk. The ratio improved to 5.55 to 1 at December 31, 1992, but increased to 7.60 to 1 at December 31, 1993. (Notice that in 1993 accounts payable, the bank line, and long-term bank debt all increased, while net worth remained exactly the same).

The high debt to worth may not be a matter for serious concern in this case. Notice that the company owes subordinated debt to Mr. Smith. Subordinated debt is considered equity (not debt) by the bank. This debt represents capital contributed by Mr. Smith, which the company cannot repay until the bank debt is repaid. When this debt is treated as equity, the ratio becomes 3.64 to 1 at December 31, 1993. This ratio remains slightly high; however, it is not extreme, and it is fairly typical for new companies.

PROFITABILITY/EFFICIENCY/ OPERATING RATIOS

Both the gross profit margin and the operating profit margin (or cushion) improved in 1992, but declined in 1993. The

Ratio Analysis

decline in 1993 could be a sign that the company is growing too rapidly. Perhaps expense control has been overlooked, while sales growth has been a priority.

Officer's compensation has increased significantly to 8.1 percent of sales in 1993. Compare this with industry averages to see if it is in line. In addition, note the values for sales to total assets, sales to net fixed assets, and sales to working capital. Compare these to industry averages to measure the company's efficiency.

Based on the financial ratios, Charlie's Chocolate Company appears to be operating within industry norms; however, several questions are raised concerning the company's financial health.

Chapter 4

CASH FLOW AND DEBT SERVICE COVERAGE ANALYSIS

INTRODUCTION TO CASH FLOW

What repays loans?

The answer is that **cash** repays loans.

The net income of a company does not repay loans; profitable businesses are frequently unable to service their debts. Collateral does not repay good loans; liquidation of collateral only repays loans in the event of default or bankruptcy. A borrower's good reputation cannot service bank debt either.

Even repayment history does not signify ability to repay loans. A borrower with a perfect repayment history may be unable to service its debts through operations. Such a borrower may rely on capital infusions, asset sales, or additional debt to service existing obligations. Conversely, a borrower that has had trouble meeting payments may only have exhibited seasonal or temporary problems.

Chapter 4

It is, therefore, necessary to measure and analyze more than the borrower's net income, collateral, reputation, or repayment history. The borrower's **cash flow from operations** must be analyzed.

THE CASH FLOWS OF THE BUSINESS ARE THE **PRIMARY** SOURCE OF REPAYMENT FOR A LOAN. FOR THIS REASON, THE CASH FLOW ANALYSIS IS THE SINGLE MOST IMPORTANT FACTOR IN DETERMINING WHETHER TO MAKE A LOAN AS WELL AS IN DETERMINING THE LOAN'S RISK.

A cash flow analysis, or debt service coverage analysis, measures cash available to service debt during historical and projected periods. Debt service **coverage** is calculated by dividing cash available by debt service required to form a ratio. Each ratio measures the percentage of debt service coverage (or how many times debt service is covered by available cash flow) for that period.

There are two types of debt service coverage ratios. The accrual basis, the "traditional" method, considers only income statement figures. The cash basis also considers changes in balance sheet accounts. The cash basis is, therefore, a true measure of **cash** available.

ACCRUAL BASIS CASH FLOW CALCULATION

The first step in the accrual basis (or traditional) cash flow analysis is to determine the net cash available to service debt. Start with **net profit** and make the following adjustments:

1. Add any non-cash expense such as **depreciation** and **amortization.** This is added because it is not an expense where cash must actually be paid. These funds are,

Cash Flow and Debt Service Coverage Analysis

therefore, available to service debt. Be sure to include depreciation which is part of the cost of sales.

2. Add **Interest Expense** because this will be considered later as part of total debt service.

3. Rent paid to company-owners (either directly or via a partnership made up of company-owners) is added back when debt service on the property being rented is also included as debt service for the company. The cash flows of the company are effectively paying the debt service on the property, but it is paid in the form of rent to the owner. (Many individuals own properties and rent to their businesses to minimize taxes by expensing the full principal and interest debt service for the company.)

Note that sometimes it is only appropriate to add back a portion of the total rent for a given period.

Example 1: If the total rent is comprised of rents for various properties, you will only add back the rent portion for the properties also owned by the owner of the company (since only that portion is considered to be debt service).

Example 2: The owner may effectively be distributing income to himself from the company through excessive rent. If the rent paid by the company is significantly more than the debt service for the given property, it may be appropriate to add back only the amount of rent necessary for debt service for the property.

Example 3: If a portion of the rent includes cash expenses such as taxes or insurance, etc., then the amounts of each of these expenses should not be added back.

Chapter 4

Note also that you should add back rent paid to owners and consider the corresponding debt service even if the loan is from a different bank. You also add back rent when the company had been renting and is now buying a facility. Be sure to include the financing of the facility in debt service.

4. **Dividends** or **withdrawals** should normally be subtracted. These are excluded if they represent distributions used to pay personal taxes on Subchapter S Corporation profits or if they represent compensation which owners rely on or are unwilling to reduce. Only if dividends or withdrawals are discretionary and are unnecessary for personal debt service or expenses, can they remain in the calculation. (See chapter on personal cash flow analysis.)

5. **Officers' salaries** may be added back if they are discretionary or will be restricted in the future. Do not, however, add back any salaries which the officers have come to rely on or are unwilling to reduce.

6. Add (subtract) any **extraordinary losses (gains)** since these are not part of the usual operations of the business. Note also that the offsetting tax effect, if any, should be added or subtracted from your adjustment.

7. Add (subtract) any **losses (gains) on the disposition of assets**. These only represent the difference between cash received for an asset and the asset's book value (book value is original cost less accumulated depreciation). Such gains and losses do not measure actual cash received or paid in asset disposition transactions. Further, these gains or losses are not a part of the regular operations of the business. For these reasons, they are excluded from the cash available calculation. (See Analysis of Capital Expenditures.) Note that the offsetting tax effect,

Cash Flow and Debt Service Coverage Analysis

if any, should be added or subtracted from your adjustment.

8. Check the most recent balance sheet to ensure that any income (or expense) producing asset still exists. If it was produced by an asset such as **a savings account, a bond, or real estate which the firm no longer owns**, then the income (or expense) should be subtracted out.

9. **Pension plan contributions and charitable contributions** are ordinarily discretionary payments. It may, therefore, be appropriate to add back some or all of these payments.

It is important to understand the concepts that determine which income and expense adjustments should be made:

1. Non-cash expenses such as depreciation should be added back.
2. Expenses such as interest or rent which will be included as required debt service should be added back.
3. Expenses (or income) which are discretionary, temporary, one-time in nature, or do not arise through regular business operations should be added back (or subtracted out).
4. If the expense or income is normal, ongoing, and has a history of occurring, then make no adjustment.

When all of the above described adjustments have been made, the sum will be the **"TOTAL AVAILABLE."**

Next, total all debt service requirements for the **upcoming** twelve months. Debt service includes both **interest and principal** payments to be made on all **proposed and existing** debt. Include all bank and finance company debt (including debt to other banks), capitalized lease payments, and officer

Chapter 4

debts with regular payments. For a line of credit, the debt service required is typically assumed to be interest only payment (zero principal payment) if the line is fully extended. The sum will be **"TOTAL DEBT SERVICE."**

Finally, calculate the **"DEBT SERVICE COVERAGE RATIO"** for each period by taking each period's **TOTAL AVAILABLE** divided by the **TOTAL DEBT SERVICE**. It is also helpful to list the **"EXCESS"** or **"DEFICIT"** coverage, which is the dollar-amount difference between each **TOTAL AVAILABLE** and the **TOTAL DEBT SERVICE**.

Note that if a period for which you calculated total cash available was only a portion of the year, then the **debt service** being considered should be multiplied by the corresponding fraction of a year.

CASH BASIS CASH FLOW

Because accrual basis cash flow analysis considers only income statement figures, it ignores many sources and uses of cash. For example, the accrual basis considers all revenues as available to service debt. What if the company you are analyzing makes a sale on credit (creating an account receivable) and does not receive cash proceeds from the sale until a later date? The proceeds from the sale are not truly available to service debt.

Conversely, what if the company incurs an expense this year which it does not actually pay until next year? The accrual basis cash flow considers this expense as cash used this year and unavailable to service this year's debts.

How can all such sources and uses of cash be considered? This is accomplished by measuring the difference between balance sheet accounts from one period to the next. For

Cash Flow and Debt Service Coverage Analysis

example, the difference between the accounts receivable balance this period and the accounts receivable balance at the end of last period represents actual **cash** collected. To make such analysis easier, there is a statement called the Statement of Cash Flows, which considers changes in balance sheet items along with income statement figures.

The cash basis cash flow is derived from the Statement of Cash Flows rather than from the income statement. It therefore considers actual cash flows rather than accrual-based performance.

CASH BASIS CASH FLOW CALCULATION

The statement labeled "Cash Flow" or "Uniform Credit Analysis (UCA) Cash Flow" on the spreadsheet program is used to analyze cash basis flow. The first step in creating a cash basis cash flow analysis is to take **net cash after operations** from the cash flow statement. Net cash after operations is the cash flow available for debt service. Make the following adjustments:

1. Add back to the figure any **rent, officers' salaries, and pension or charitable contributions** if they were added back for the accrual basis cash flow.

2. Subtract dividends or withdrawals if they were subtracted for the accrual basis cash flow.

3. Adjust for any **extraordinary gains or losses**. These are included in "miscellaneous cash income" preceding net cash after operations on the cash flow statement.

Chapter 4

The remaining sum is the **TOTAL AVAILABLE**. From this point, the calculations are the same as for the accrual based cash flow. The debt service is the same, and the calculations of coverage ratios are the same.

It is important to understand why it is not necessary to perform certain add-backs when calculating the cash basis cash available:

1. Depreciation and amortization are non-cash expenses; so they do not appear on cash flow statements. Since these expenses are excluded from the statement, they do not need to be added back.

2. Interest expense is not added back since it has not yet been subtracted on the "net cash after operations" line in the cash flow statement. (If interest expense is listed above the line used for cash available, then it should be added back.)

3. No adjustments are made for gains or losses on sales of assets because they also have not yet been considered as part of "net cash after operations." Notice that these cash flows are inherent in the "capital expenditures" line, which is further below in the investing section of the cash flow statement.

ANALYSIS OF DEBT SERVICE COVERAGE

Obviously, a 1:1 coverage of debt service is adequate to pay debts; however, as an extra margin of comfort, the bank may only consider debt service coverage of at least 1.2:1 (or 1.2 times) to be acceptable. Double coverage (2.0 times or better) is generally required to make a loan a "superior" risk.

ANALYSIS OF ACCRUAL VERSUS CASH BASIS

The amount of debt coverage will almost always differ between cash basis and accrual basis cash flows for a given period. The cause of these differences can be deduced by analyzing the statement of cash flows.

The operating portion of the statement of cash flows considers sales, cost of sales, and expenses as does the income statement. However, the statement of cash flows also considers changes in various balance sheet items between the end of the current period and the end of the previous period. The changes in receivables, payables, inventory, and prepaids/deferreds are what cause cash basis cash available to be different from accrual basis cash available.

On the statement of cash flows, a positive number is a **source** of funds or a source of cash added to total net cash after operations. A negative number is a **use** of cash or a subtraction to get net cash after operations.

So, for example, an increase in receivables is a **use** of cash; it causes the cash basis cash available to be less than accrual basis cash available. An increase in inventory is also a **use** of cash causing the cash basis cash flow figure to be less favorable than the accrual basis. An increase in payables is, however, a **source** of cash. This causes, all things being equal, a more favorable cash basis than accrual basis.

The above factors are called **swing factors** (as opposed to **fundamental factors** such as profit margins). Swing factors are analyzed in the cash basis cash flow but not in the accrual basis cash flow. Swing factors have an impact on cumulative cash flow which is over and above revenues and expenses measured by the accrual basis cash available.

Chapter 4

IMPACTS UPON CASH FLOW

Note that both changes in revenue and changes in turnover from period to period impact cash flow. For example, either sales increase with constant inventory turnover or decreased inventory turnover with sales remaining constant will cause a **use** of cash.

It should also be noted that a growing firm will typically absorb cash even as sales increase and the firm is profitable. This occurs because of the swing factors. For example, growing sales may require large inventory purchases which use cash. Growing sales on credit also use cash. In fact, even if accounts receivable turnover remains constant, sales growth causes cash to be used to finance the dollar growth in receivables. The result of these effects is that cash basis cash flow is less favorable than accrual basis cash flow for the growing firm.

SUMMARY OF SOURCES AND USES OF CASH

Sources of funds:

    Revenue/Income on the Income Statement
    Decrease in Assets
    Increase in Liabilities
    Increase in Equity

Uses of funds:

    Expense/Loss on the Income Statement
    Increase in Assets
    Decrease in Liabilities
    Decrease in Equity

See Exhibits 4.1 and 4.2.

Cash Flow and Debt Service Coverage Analysis

Exhibit 4.1 SUMMARY OF CASH AVAILABLE CALCULATIONS

Accrual basis cash available adjustments to **net income:**

Add	Depreciation or Amortization	Always
Add	Interest Expense	Always
Add	Rent Paid to Company Owners	Usually
Subtract	Dividends or Withdrawals	Usually
Add	Officer Salaries	Sometimes
Add	Extraordinary Losses	Always
Subtract	Extraordinary Gains	Always
Add	Losses on the Disposition of Assets	Usually
Subtract	Gains on the Disposition of Assets	Usually

Exhibit 4.2
Cash basis cash flow adjustments to **Net Cash After Operations:**

Add	Rent Paid to Company Owners	Usually
Add	Officer Salaries	Sometimes
Subtract	Dividends or Withdrawals	Usually
Add	Extraordinary Losses	Always
Subtract	Extraordinary Gains	Always
Add	Pension Plan or Charitable Contributions	Sometimes

Chapter 4

ANALYSIS OF CAPITAL EXPENDITURES

Capital expenditures or upcoming capital expenditures can affect debt service ability. Here are a few ways to measure the effects of fixed asset purchases on cash flow:

1. Examine the "Investing" section of the statement of cash flows. This section summarizes all fixed assets sales and purchases. Unlike gains/losses on disposition of assets on the income statement, this section represents actual cash flows since it excludes depreciation expense.

2. Consider calculations with some portion of depreciation expense subtracted from the cash available, since depreciation represents a "using up" of fixed assets. It may be appropriate to subtract depreciation from cash available to the extent that it represents a realistic usage of the life of the asset.

3. Ask the borrower what fixed asset transactions are anticipated in the near future, or estimate them yourself. Fixed asset transactions along with their anticipated financing transactions are used in projections.

Keep in mind, that when a fixed asset will be purchased with financing, only the down payment represents cash used. The remainder represents future debt service to be paid for through the operations of the firm.

Cash Flow and Debt Service Coverage Analysis

CASE STUDY: CASH FLOW ANALYSIS OF CHARLIE'S CHOCOLATE COMPANY

The calculation of the **TOTAL AVAILABLE** values is as follows: (in thousands)

	1991	1992	1993
Accrual Basis:			
Net Profit	($ 26)	$ 23	$ 10
Add: Deprec. in COGS	$ 25	$ 25	$ 30
Add: Depreciation	$ 0	$ 25	$ 25
Add: Amortization	$ 5	$ 5	$ 5
Add: Interest Exp.	$ 2	$ 27	$ 36
Add: Rent Expense	$100	$100	$110
Add: Charitable Cont.	–0–	–0–	$ 10
Less: Gain /Asset sale	–0–	–0–	($ 12)
Less: Dividends	–0–	($ 5)	($ 10)
TOTAL AVAILABLE	$135	$200	$ 204
Cash Basis:			
Net Cash After Oper.	N/A	15	($ 88)
Add: Rent Expense	N/A	$100	$110
Add: Charitable Cont.	N/A	–0–	$ 10
Less: Dividends	N/A	($ 5)	($ 10)
TOTAL AVAILABLE	N/A	$110	$ 22

Next calculate **TOTAL EXISTING ANNUAL DEBT SERVICE**: (in thousands)

Chapter 4

Annual Payment	Loan:	Description of payment:
$ 47	$230 Bank Term Note	Monthly principal payments of $2,500 plus interest accrued at 8%.
$ 20	$58 Bank Term Note	Monthly principal and interest payments of $1,657.
$ 86	$500 Commercial Mortgage	Monthly principal payments of $4,167 plus interest accrued at 8%.
$ 8	$100 Line of Credit	Monthly interest only payments at 8%. Assume that the line of credit is fully drawn.
$ 8	$75 Officer Loan	Interest only payments at 10%.
$169	**TOTAL DEBT SERVICE REQUIRED**	

It is now possible to calculate the **DEBT SERVICE COVERAGE RATIOS** and the **EXCESS/DEFICIT** amounts: (in thousands)

	1991	1992	1993
Accrual Basis:			
Total Accrual Avail.	$ 135	$200	$204
Total Debt Service	$ 169	$169	$169
Debt Coverage Ratio	0.80x	1.18x	1.21x
Excess / (deficit)	($ 34)	$ 31	$ 35
Cash Basis:			
Total Accrual Avail.	N/A	$110	$ 22
Total Debt Service	N/A	$169	$169
Debt Coverage Ratio	N/A	0.65x	0.13x
Excess / (deficit)	N/A	($ 59)	($147)

Cash Flow and Debt Service Coverage Analysis

ANALYSIS

On an accrual basis, the company shows the ability to service its debts. Debt service coverage is approximately 1.20 times (or 120 percent) in 1992 and 1993. In fact, there is an extra cushion of over $30,000 during these years.

When cash flows from changes in receivable, payable, inventory, and prepaid/accrual balances are included in the calculation, there is significantly less cash available. The company is unable to service its debt in 1992 and 1993 as measured by the cash basis cash flow. The shortages are $59,000 in 1992 and $147,000 in 1993.

Analyze the cash flow statement to determine which factors contributed to the deficit debt service coverage for 1992. In 1992, receivables rose by $56,000 and inventories rose by $32,000. The increases in these two accounts **used** a total of $88,000 in cash and were the primary reason for the deficit coverage. Notice that although sales increases, decreases in turnover rates contributed to the use of cash.

Which factors contributed to the deficit coverage in 1993? Again, the receivable and inventory balances increased dramatically for a total $227,000 **use** of cash. Again, receivable and inventory turnover rates decreased. This implies that not only was the $227,000 in cash used to finance increasing sales, but that it was used to finance slower inventory turnover and slower collection of receivables. Inventory increased at a higher rate than sales increased; this is unhealthy.

In 1993, however, the payables balance also increased for a $58,000 **source** of cash. The payables increase offsets a portion of the use of cash for receivables and inventory.

The extension of the payables balance in 1993 is not healthy; in fact, it is a sign of potential trouble. The company's line of credit is fully drawn, but they still need cash. Consequently, the company has extended payables (payables turnover increased), and they have even overdrawn their bank

Chapter 4

account. (Perhaps the company needs a larger line of credit to avoid this.)

New and growing companies typically absorb cash even though they are profitable. Inventory needs to be built up for growing sales, and receivables build up as more and more sales are made. Charlie's Chocolate Company is an example of a profitable, growing company in need of cash.

The main difference between Charlie's Chocolate Company and a healthy, growing company is that the turnover ratios, particularly inventory turnover, are slowing significantly. Inventory should be scaled back, particularly since it is comprised of food products which cannot be stored for long periods of time. This action, along with a possible extension of increased short-term bank borrowings will help improve the company's cash position in 1994.

Chapter 5

ASSESSING BUSINESS PLANS AND MANAGEMENT ABILITY

BUSINESS PLANS

Commercial loan borrowers and applicants should provide the bank with information beyond historical financial data. Information, including a business plan and projections, is necessary to make informed loan decisions; it is an essential part of commercial loan analysis.

A "business plan" is a detailed description of a business and its strategies. It is necessary both as a management tool and as a vehicle to procure financing. A business plan starts with a "mission." The mission statement describes, in general terms, the market or the goal of the business. It should describe, specifically, what need the business satisfies in the marketplace. For example, the mission of Charlie's Chocolate Company is, "to provide a complete line of fine chocolates for true chocolate lovers."

The mission statement should be supported by detailed descriptions, plans, and goals. It is also essential that each

Chapter 5

goal be supported by a description of who will be responsible for seeing that the goal is met plus how he or she will accomplish it. The entire plan should be updated at least annually by the borrower, and the plan should be supplied to the bank as soon as it becomes available.

TOPICS THAT A BUSINESS PLAN SHOULD ADDRESS

>   Strengths
>   Weaknesses
>   Opportunities
>   Threats
>   Competitors
>   Customers
>   Large concentrations of sales to specific customers
>   Product descriptions
>   Research and development
>   Market definition
>   Market size
>   Market share
>   Pricing
>   Marketing
>   Advertising
>   Mission
>   Sales goals
>   Cost cutting goals
>   Operational goals
>   Specific plans for achieving each goal, including **who** will be esponsible
>   Industry analysis
>   Local market analysis
>   Location
>   Seasonality of business

Assessing Business Plans and Management Ability

Cyclical nature of business
Key employees
Management structure
Management succession
Management strengths and weaknesses

MANAGEMENT ABILITY

The primary concern in assessing the ability of management is the general operation of the business. The bank is concerned with how well management understands its market and its competition, not necessarily how familiar management is with banking and finance.

One measure of management ability is experience or time spent in the industry. However, the best measure may be the extent that sound business plans and strategies are in place, and how well the business is structured and organized to meet the objectives.

Chapter 6

ANALYZING PROJECTIONS

ANALYZING PROJECTIONS

Projections are another essential element of credit analysis. After all, it is the **future** cash flow of the firm that will repay the debt.

Since projections represent the **financial** plans and goals of the firm, they should be supported by descriptions of how they will be met and who will be responsible for meeting them. In addition, assumptions such as economic conditions made to construct projections should be included.

It is typically necessary for the analyst or loan officer to formulate projections himself or herself if the borrower does not supply them. (Most spreadsheet programs have projection capabilities which make the process easy.) Bank projections are also necessary if the bank has different assumptions than the borrower or if the bank receives only projected income statements. Finally, the bank may also formulate its own projections to perform **sensitivity analysis**.

Sensitivity analysis is the alteration of one or two variables in a projection to examine its effects. The sensitivity to

Chapter 6

the changing of the variable is measured. For example, the bank may examine a borrower's sensitivity to a 10 percent decrease in sales. The analyst or loan officer would examine how the change in sales, in turn, changes the cash flows and repayment ability of the borrower. Any variables, including income, expenses, balance sheet items, fixed asset purchases, turnover ratios, or financing changes can be altered to measure sensitivity.

CASE STUDY: FINANCIAL PROJECTIONS FOR CHARLIE'S CHOCOLATE COMPANY

Once historical financial statements have been analyzed, it is appropriate to formulate projections. Historical figures, especially those from fiscal year-ended December 31, 1993, are the basis for projections in this example. A sample of possible assumptions for 1994 projections follows:

1. Assume sales growth is expected to continue at the 1993 rate. Project 35 percent for sales growth in 1994.
2. Assume that Mr. Smith contractually agrees to limit officers' compensation in 1994. Project $90,000 for 1994 officers' compensation.
3. Since Charlie's Chocolate Company is a Subchapter S Corporation, Mr. Smith pays taxes personally on the company's profits. Assume that dividends for 1994 will equal Mr. Smith's personal tax on the net income of the company. This allows Mr. Smith to pay the tax with company funds.
4. Assume that interest rates will remain the same.

Analyzing Projections

5. Assume that inventory turnover will speed up since this has become a concern. Project 99 days for inventory turnover in 1994.

6. Assume that receivables turnover will improve slightly in 1993. Project 73 days for inventory turnover in 1994.

7. Assume that potential cash from receivables and inventory will allow payables turnover to speed up slightly. Project 50 days for payables turnover in 1994.

8. The company needs to replace one piece of mixing equipment. Assume that the company will make a fixed asset purchase of $50,000 in 1994 for the equipment. Assume that the company will put $10,000 down, and that the bank will finance the $40,000 balance.

After assumptions are made and projected data is entered into the spreadsheet program, the statements should be analyzed in the same way as historical figures. See Exhibits 6.1 to 6.5 for the projected financial statements for Charlie's Chocolate Company.

ANALYZING PROJECTIONS

Pay particular attention to projected debt service ability, since **this is what will actually repay the bank's loans**. Based on the projections, the company has accrual cash available of $244,000 and cash basis cash available of $243,000. Both figures cover debt service requirements.

Based on the projections, the company needs an additional line of credit to operate. Even though turnover ratios and cash flow are expected to improve, the short-term borrowing need at December 31, 1994 will be $110,000. This need exceeds the company's current line of credit commit-

Chapter 6

Exhibit 6.1

```
                CHARLIE'S CHOCOLATE COMPANY, INC./PROJECTIONS
FAST 4.3                  Common Size Report                    02/25/94
General Industries         1994 PROJECTION                      01:30 P.M.

SIC Code : 2064_
Auditor : Ryan Jones, CPA        CPA PRP
Analyst : Ken Pirok              Dec 31          FORCST
Base = Last Actual                1993            1994
AMOUNTS IN THOUSANDS OF DOLLARS   12 Mth
=========================================================================
COMMON SIZE REPORT                  $       %       $       %
=========================================================================
ASSETS:
-------------------------------------------------------------------------

    Accounts Receivable - Trade    277    35.9    348    44.7

    Raw Materials                  266    34.5    214    27.4
    Finished Goods                  32     4.1     26     3.3
                                   -----------    -----------
Total Inventory                    298    38.6    239    30.7

                                   -----------    -----------
    TOTAL CURRENT ASSETS           575    74.5    588    75.4

    Machinery & Equipment          280    36.3    327    42.0
    Transportation Equipment        15     1.9     18     2.3
                                   -----------    -----------
Gross Fixed Assets                 295    38.2    345    44.3
less: Accumulated Depreciation     164    21.2    228    29.3
                                   -----------    -----------
Total Fixed Assets - Net           131    17.0    117    15.0

Due from Employees                  12     1.6     12     1.5

Prepaid Expenses - Non Current      39     5.1     53     6.8

       INTANGIBLES
    Goodwill - Net                  15     1.9     10     1.3
                                   -----------    -----------
NON-CURRENT ASSETS                 197    25.5    191    24.6
                                   -----------    -----------
    TOTAL ASSETS                   772   100.0    779   100.0
=========================================================================
```

Analyzing Projections

Exhibit 6.2

```
              CHARLIE'S CHOCOLATE COMPANY, INC./PROJECTIONS
FAST 4.3              Common Size Report              02/25/94
General Industries     1994 PROJECTION                01:30 P.M.

SIC Code : 2064_
Auditor : Ryan Jones, CPA         CPA PRP
Analyst : Ken Pirok               Dec 31         FORCST
Base = Last Actual                 1993           1994
AMOUNTS IN THOUSANDS OF DOLLARS   12 Mth
==========================================================  ==============
     LIABILITIES                   $        %       $       %
```

LIABILITIES	$	%	$	%
Overdraft	41	5.3	......	......
Notes Payable S/T - Bank	100	13.0	100	12.8
Additional Short Term Debt	......	......	10	1.3
Current Maturities LTD - 1	40	5.2	40	5.1
Accounts Payable - Trade	103	13.3	121	15.5
Wages/Salaries Payable	19	2.5	26	3.3
Interest Payable	3	0.4	4	0.5
Total Accrued Liabilities	22	2.8	30	3.8
TOTAL CURRENT LIABILITIES	306	39.6	300	38.6
Exist Long Term Debt - 1	288	37.3	248	31.8
New Long Term Debt - 1	......	......	40	5.1
TOTAL SENIOR LT LIABILITIES	288	37.3	288	37.0
TOTAL SENIOR LIABILITIES	594	76.9	588	75.5
Subordinated Debt - 1	75	9.7	75	9.6
TOTAL LIABILITIES	669	86.7	663	85.1

NET WORTH

	$	%	$	%
Common Stock	1	0.1	1	0.1
Paid In Capital	99	12.8	99	12.7
Retained Earnings	3	0.4	16	2.0
NET WORTH	103	13.3	116	14.9
TOTAL LIABILITIES & NET WORTH	772	100.0	779	100.0
Tangible Net Worth	88	11.4	106	13.6
Working Capital	269	34.8	287	36.9

67

Chapter 6

Exhibit 6.3

```
                  CHARLIE'S CHOCOLATE COMPANY, INC./PROJECTIONS
FAST 4.3                    Common Size Report                   02/25/94
General Industries          1994 PROJECTION                      01:30 P.M.

SIC Code : 2064_
Auditor : Ryan Jones, CPA        CPA PRP
Analyst : Ken Pirok              Dec 31          FORCST
Base = Last Actual               1993            1994
AMOUNTS IN THOUSANDS OF DOLLARS  12 Mth
==========================================================================
       INCOME  STATEMENT          $        %        $        %

     Sales (Product 1)          1,290    100.0    1,742    100.0

Cost of Goods Sold (Product 1)    654     50.7      883     50.7
Depreciation in CoGS               30      2.3       35      2.0
                                 -----------------------------------
     GROSS PROFIT/REVENUES        606     47.0      824     47.3

General & Administrative Expense  301     23.3      492     25.4
Officers Compensation             105      8.1       90      5.2
Lease & Rental Expense            110      8.5      110      9.3
Bad Debt Expense                   16      1.2       26      1.4
Depreciation                       25      1.9       29      1.7
Amortization                        5      0.4        5      0.3
                                 -----------------------------------
     TOTAL OPERATING EXPENSES     562     43.6      752     43.2
                                 -----------------------------------
     OPERATING INCOME              44      3.4       71      4.1

Interest Expense ST                36      2.8       42      2.4
                                 -----------------------------------
     TOTAL INTEREST EXPENSE        36      2.8       42      2.4

Gain on Sale of Assets             12      0.9    .......  .......
Charitable Contributions           10      0.8       10      0.6
                                 -----------------------------------
     NET PROFIT                    10      0.8       19      1.1

Cash Dividend - Common Stock       10      0.8        6      0.3
                                 -----------------------------------
     CHANGE IN NET WORTH       .......  .......      13      0.7
==========================================================================
```

Analyzing Projections

Exhibit 6.4

```
CHARLIE'S CHOCOLATE COMPANY, INC./PROJECTIONS
FAST 4.3          Cash Flow          02/25/94
General Industries  1994 PROJECTI...  01:30 P.M.

SIC Code : 2064_
Auditor : Ryan Jones, CPA
Analyst : Ken Pirok                    FORCST
Base = Last Actual                      1994
AMOUNTS IN THOUSANDS OF DOLLARS
==================================================
C A S H F L O W
--------------------------------------------------
Sales - Net                             1,742
Change in Receivables                     -71
                                      --------
CASH FROM SALES                         1,670

Cost of Goods Sold                       -883
Change in Inventories                      59
Change in Payables                         18
                                      --------
CASH PRODUCTION COSTS                    -806
                                      --------
GROSS CASH PROFITS                        864

SG & A Expense                           -718
Change in Prepaids                        -14
Change in Accruals                          7
                                      --------
Cash Operating Expense                   -725
                                      --------
CASH AFTER OPERATIONS                     139

Miscellaneous Cash Income                 -10
                                      --------
NET CASH AFTER OPERATIONS                 129

Interest Expense                          -41
Dividends Paid                             -6
                                      --------
Financing Costs                           -47

NET CASH INCOME                            81

Current Portion Long Term Debt            -40
                                      --------
CASH AFTER DEBT AMORTIZATION               41

Capital Expenditures - Tangible           -50
                                      --------
FINANCING SURPLUS/(REQUIREMENTS)           -9

Change in Short Term Debt                 -31
Change in Long Term Debt                   40
                                      --------
Total External Financing                    9
                                      --------
Cash After Financing                       -0
==================================================
Net Income + Depreciation                  88

Misc Cash Income Detail:
Other Expense                             -10
                                      --------
Total                                     -10
==================================================
```

Chapter 6

Exhibit 6.5

```
              CHARLIE'S CHOCOLATE COMPANY, INC./PROJECTIONS
    FAST 4.3              Financial Ratios           02/25/94
    General Industries    1994 PROJECTION            01:30 P.M.

    SIC Code : 2064
    Auditor : Ryan Jones, CPA
    Analyst : Ken Pirok                     CPA PRP
    Base = Last Actual                      Dec 31   FORCST
    AMOUNTS IN THOUSANDS OF DOLLARS          1993     1994
                                            12 Mth
    =========================================================
    F I N A N C I A L    R A T I O S
    ---------------------------------------------------------
    GROWTH RATIOS:
    Net Sales Growth, Composite %            N/A      35.00
      Sales Growth, Sales (Product 1)        N/A      35.00
    Net Income Growth, %                     N/A      87.44
    Total Assets Growth, %                   N/A       0.92
    Total Liabilities Growth, %              N/A      -0.85
    Net Worth Growth, %                      N/A      12.37
    ---------------------------------------------------------
    PROFITABILITY RATIOS:
    Gross Margin, Composite %               49.30     49.30
      Margin, Sales (Product 1)             49.30     49.30
    SG & A, %                               41.24     41.24
    Cushion (Gross Margin - SG & A), %       8.06      8.06
    Depreciation, Amortization, %            4.65      3.98
    Operating Profit Margin, %               3.41      4.08
    Interest Expense, %                      2.79      2.43
    Operating Margin, %                      0.62      1.65
    Net Margin, %                            0.78      1.08
    Return on Average Assets, %              N/A       2.42
    Return on Average Equity, %              N/A      19.35
    Dividend Payout Rate, %                100.00     32.01
    ---------------------------------------------------------
    COVERAGE RATIOS:
    EBITDA / (Total Interest + CMLTD)        N/A       1.58
    Interest Coverage (EBIT / Interest)      1.28      1.44
    Net Income + Depreciation / CMLTD        N/A       2.20
    ---------------------------------------------------------
    ACTIVITY RATIOS:
    Receivables in Days                       78        73
    Inventory in Days                        166        99
    Payables in Days                          57        50
    Total Assets / Net sales                 0.60      0.45
    ---------------------------------------------------------
    LIQUIDITY RATIOS:
    Working Capital                          269       287
    Quick Ratio                             0.91      1.16
    Current Ratio                           1.88      1.96
    Sales / Net Working Capital             4.80      6.06
    ---------------------------------------------------------
    LEVERAGE RATIOS:
    Total Liabilities / T Net Worth         7.60      6.27
    Tot Sr. Liabs. / TNW & Sub Debt         3.64      3.26
    Borrowed Funds / TNW & Sub Debt         2.88      2.42
    Long-Term Debt / Net Fixed Assets       2.50      2.81
    ---------------------------------------------------------
    CASH POSITION:
    Cash Margin                   %          N/A      49.60
    Cash Coverage                            N/A       1.47
    Net Cash Income                          N/A        81
    Net Income + Depreciation                 70        88
    ---------------------------------------------------------
    SUSTAINABLE GROWTH & BANKRUPTCY:
    Sustainable Growth, (N/(T-N))  %       .......    7.48
    Z=1.2x1 +1.4x2 +3.3x3 +.6x4 +.999x5      2.38      3.07
    =========================================================
```

Analyzing Projections

ment of $100,000, and it does not consider fluctuations such as seasonal needs which may arise during the year.

Try changing some of the variables to measure sensitivity. For example, if sales grow by 20 percent (as they did in 1992), how will this affect repayment ability and profits? If profit margins decline by one percent or if interest rates increase, what will happen to repayment ability and profits?

Chapter 7

ANALYZING PERSONAL FINANCIAL STATEMENTS

PERSONAL FINANCIAL STATEMENTS

The personal financial statement is nothing more than a balance sheet for an individual. The statement represents a point in time just like a business balance sheet. The primary difference between the two types of balance sheets is that a business balance sheet classifies assets, for the most part, at historical cost, while a personal financial statement generally classifies assets at market value. Another difference is that the personal financial statement is usually completed by the individual on a form supplied by the bank instead of by an accountant. Because of this, it is crucial that the individual sign the statement.

    The personal financial statement is analyzed for individual borrowers and for guarantors. The analysis focuses on determining how much additional support the borrower or guarantor provides to a commercial loan. To measure additional support, the analyst calculates **adjusted net worth** and **total liquid assets**.

Chapter 7

ADJUSTED NET-WORTH CALCULATION

Since the goal of analyzing the individual's personal financial statement is to measure **additional support** over and above that of the company, adjustments must be made. The concept behind adjusting stated net worth is to accurately measure the value of the individual's assets net of liabilities, and **exclusive** of the particular business or project that is being analyzed. To calculate adjusted net worth, **begin with stated net worth** and make the following adjustments:

1. Subtract the value of the individual's business as stated on the asset side of the personal financial statement. (Also, **add** any debts **in the name of the business** which may occasionally appear as personal liabilities.)

2. Subtract loans due to the individual from the business.

3. Adjust for any changes which have occurred to the stated value of marketable securities. It is appropriate to look these values up yourself to obtain an accurate, up-to-date value.

4. Subtract personal assets, such as art collections or jewelry, which may be of questionable value or may be difficult to liquidate.

5. Verify that the individual reports **cash value of life insurance** not face value. **Adjust** the stated value if necessary.

6. Check the individual's credit bureau report to verify that all existing liabilities have been reported. **Adjust** for any unreported liabilities.

Analyzing Personal Financial Statements

CALCULATION OF TOTAL LIQUID ASSETS

Liquid assets include cash, certificates of deposit, U.S. Government securities, and marketable securities. Liquid assets exclude equity in closely held companies and in unlisted securities. Liquid assets also typically exclude the cash value of life insurance and IRA accounts.

CASE STUDY: CHARLES SMITH'S PERSONAL FINANCIAL STATEMENT

The personal financial statement completed by Mr. Smith comprises Exhibit 7.1, pages 1 and 2.

CALCULATION OF ADJUSTED NET WORTH

Begin with Mr. Smith's **stated net worth of $1,108,300**.

Subtract the value of the company, which is stated at **$200,000**.

Subtract the loan receivable from the company of $75,000.

Subtract the personal property of $10,000 since it consists of assets which are of questionable value.

Note that Mr. Smith reports $500,000 as the **cash value** of life insurance on page one of the statement, while, on page two, he reports $500,000 as the face value. Assume you learn

Chapter 7

Exhibit 7.1 PERSONAL FINANCIAL STATEMENT

DATE: February 25, 1994   Page 1

APPLICANT		CO-APPLICANT	
NAME	Charles C. Smith	NAME	
ADDRESS	1234 Chocolate Bar	ADDRESS	
	Candyland, IL 00000		
PHONE	217-555-0000	PHONE	
OCCUPATION	Candy Maker	OCCUPATION	
BUSINESS ADDRESS		BUSINESS ADDRESS	
	1000 E. Debra		
	Candyland, IL 00000		
BUSINESS PHONE	217-555-0000	BUSINESS PHONE	

ASSETS	AMOUNT	LIABILITIES	AMOUNT
CASH ON HAND		NOTES PAYABLE TO BANKS	$650,000
CASH IN BANKS	$500	ACCOUNTS/NOTES PAYABLE	$2,000
U.S. GOVT. SECURITIES		OTHER PAYABLES	
MARKETABLE SECURITIES	$25,000	TAXES PAYABLE	$200
NON-MARETABLE SECURITIES	$200,000	AUTOMOBILE DEBTS	$5,000
ACCOUNTS/NOTES RECEIVABLE	$75,000	CREDIT CARDS	$5,000
REAL ESTATE OWNED	$950,000	OTHER LIABILITIES	
AUTOMOBILES	$10,000		
PERSONAL PROPERTY	$10,000		
CASH VALUE OF LIFE INS.	$500,000		
OTHER ASSETS			
		TOTAL LIABILITIES	662,200
		NET WORTH	1,108,300
TOTAL ASSETS	1,770,500	TOTAL LIAB. & NET WORTH	1,770,550

Analyzing Personal Financial Statements

Exhibit 7.1 PERSONAL FINANCIAL STATEMENT
(continued)

DATE: February 25, 1994   Page 2

NAME	NUMBER OF SHARES	MARKET VALUE
Municipal Bonds	25	$ 25,000
Charlie's Chocolate Company, Inc.	1,000	$200,000

REAL ESTATE:

ADDRESS	COST	MARKET VALUE	MORT. BALANCE
1000 E. Debra	$675,000	$750,000	$500,000
50 North Shore	$ 75,000	$ 75,000	$ 50,000
1234 Chocolate Bar	$130,000	$125,000	$100,000

OTHER ASSETS:

NAME	VALUE	LOAN BALANCE
Note receivable from company	$ 75,000	N/A
1993 Ford Thunderbird	$ 10,000	$5,000
Books, Art, Antiques	$ 10,000	N/A
Life insurance (face value)	$500,000	N/A

REVOLVING DEBT/ACCOUNTS & NOTES PAYABLE/OTHER LIABILITIES:

NAME	AMOUNT DUE
Ryan Jones	$2,000
Income Tax	$ 200
Visa	$5,000

SIGNATURE: _____ DATE: _____
SIGNATURE: _____ DATE: _____

Chapter 7

that $500,000 is the **face value** and that **$5,000 is the cash value**. You should, therefore, **subtract** $500,000 minus $5,000 or **$495,000** from net worth.

The adjusted net worth calculation is summarized as follows:

Stated Net Worth	$1,108,300
Less: Value of Company	$ 200,000
Less: Loan Receivable from Company	$ 75,000
Less: Personal Property	$ 10,000
Less: Cash Value of Life Insurance Adjustment	$ 495,000
ADJUSTED PERSONAL NET WORTH	$ 328,300

ANALYSIS OF ADJUSTED NET WORTH AND TOTAL LIQUID ASSETS

You can infer that Mr. Smith personally provides $328,300 in additional support to the loan relationship. This support is in the form of personal equity over and above the resources of the company.

It is, however, inaccurate to conclude that Mr. Smith could provide this entire equity amount for support, since most of the equity is in the form of real estate. Such assets would not be easy to liquidate, especially at stated market value. It is, therefore, necessary to measure liquid assets to learn which assets could be easily liquidated. For Mr. Smith, these assets include cash in banks and marketable securities for **total liquid assets of $25,500**.

Finally, note that the statement is unsigned. It is crucial that the bank ask Mr. Smith to sign the statement or to prepare a new one.

Chapter 8

PERSONAL CASH FLOW ANALYSIS

INTRODUCTION

Personal cash flow analysis is typically necessary for the following reasons:

1. Determining the ability of individual borrowers to repay loans made to them personally.
2. Determining the amount of officer salaries or owner distributions that are necessary to service personal debts (or expenses such as taxes). This allows the analyst to determine how much, if any, of these salaries or distributions are discretionary and can thus be included in the **company's** cash available calculations.
3. Determining how much extra support a guarantor provides.

Determination of personal cash flows is usually achieved by analyzing personal tax returns. Since they include many non-cash expenses and exclude many cash income and expense items, it is important to strictly examine the tax returns.

Chapter 8

When requesting tax returns, be sure to specify that **all** schedules should be included. This will enable you to perform a thorough analysis.

PERSONAL CASH AVAILABLE CALCULATION

Start with **"total income"** which is **line 23** of the Form 1040. (Note that the **"adjustments to income"** section below this line includes non-cash and discretionary expenses. For this reason, none of these will be considered in the calculation of cash available. Also note, however, that if any alimony is paid (line 29) and is expected to continue, then it should be included later as a debt service requirement.) Make the following adjustments to **total income**:

1. Subtract any **other income** (line 22) if it is one-time in nature, or if it is not expected to continue in the future (for example, gambling winnings).

   If this income has a history of receipt and is expected to continue in the future (for example, continuing fee income), then **make no adjustment** to **include** it.

2. Add back all **other loss** items (line 22). These include state tax adjustments, foreign income adjustments, and loss carry-forwards, all of which do not affect personal cash flow.

3. If **social security benefits** (line 21) are expected to continue, then they should be included in cash available. To **include** them, **subtract line 21b, and add back line**

Personal Cash Flow Analysis

21a. (This will ensure that you include **all** social security benefits received, not just the taxable portion.)

If social security benefits are **not expected to continue**, then simply **subtract line 21b**.

4. Business or farm income or loss (lines 12 and 19) can be **excluded** by **subtracting** the corresponding line. Exclude these cash flows if they are non-recurring or if you construct a separate business cash flow analysis.

   If you do include these cash flows, be sure to add back depreciation, add back interest expense, subtract non-tax deductible meal and entertainment expense, and add back casualty loss (fire, flood loss, etc.).

5. Rents, royalties, partnerships, estates, trusts, etc. (line 18) should be analyzed by examining schedule E. To **include** the cash income and expenses for a **property** do the following:
   a. Subtract line 26 of the schedule E.
   b. Subtract line 19 of the schedule E. These are cash expenses.
   c. Add line 12 of the schedule E. This represents interest expense. Since you are including this property's income/expenses in the personal cash flow, this interest expense will be included later in the debt service calculation.
   d. Add line 3 of the schedule E. These are cash revenues.

   To **exclude** a property, simply **subtract line 26** of the schedule E. If there are multiple properties, only make

Chapter 8

the above adjustments for the properties which you intend to include.

6. Examine Part II of the Schedule E to uncover partnership or S Corporation income or loss. Line 31 on page 2 of the Schedule E lists the total income or loss. This income or loss is "passed through" to the individual for tax purposes; however, it does not represent actual cash flow. **Subtract line 31 of the Schedule E.**

For an **S Corporation**, dividends and distributions to the owners as well as capital contributions to the company do represent actual cash flows. To determine the amount of such dividends, distributions, or contributions, examine **company** financial statements or tax returns. **Add any dividends or distributions and subtract any contributions** from personal cash available.

For a **partnership**, examine the Schedule K-1 (Form 1065: "Partner's Share of Income, Credits, Deductions, Etc."), which will be included to determine actual cash flows. **Perform steps a through c below**:

   a. Subtract Box b (capital contributed during year) since this represents actual cash paid.

   b. Add Box d (withdrawals and distributions) since this represents actual cash received.

   c. Add line 5 (guaranteed payments to partner) since this is regular compensation guaranteed to continue.

7. Pensions and annuities and IRA distributions (lines 16 and 17) are included in cash available if they are expected to continue. To **include** them, **subtract the b line and add back the a line** to ensure that all cash flows (includ-

Personal Cash Flow Analysis

CASE STUDY: ANALYZING MR. SMITH'S PERSONAL TAX RETURN

Mr. Smith's personal tax return for 1992 comprises Exhibits 8.1 to 8.6. A personal cash flow construction follows.

Exhibit 8.1 Form 1040–U.S. Individual Income Tax Return

Form 1040 — Department of the Treasury—Internal Revenue Service
U.S. Individual Income Tax Return 1992
OMB No. 1545-0074

Label
Your first name and initial: CHARLES C.   Last name: SMITH
Your social security number: 000:00:0000
Home address: 1234 CHOCOLATE BAR
City, town or post office, state, and ZIP code: CANDYLAND, IL 00000

Presidential Election Campaign: Do you want $1 to go to this fund? Yes / **No** (checked)
If a joint return, does your spouse want $1 to go to this fund? Yes / **No** (checked)

Filing Status
1. [X] Single
2. [ ] Married filing joint return
3. [ ] Married filing separate return
4. [ ] Head of household
5. [ ] Qualifying widow(er)

Exemptions
6a. [X] Yourself
6b. [ ] Spouse
No. of boxes checked on 6a and 6b: **1**
No. of your children on 6c who lived with you: 0
didn't live with you due to divorce or separation: 0
No. of other dependents on 6c: 0
Total number of exemptions claimed: **1**

Income

7	Wages, salaries, tips, etc. Attach Form(s) W-2	50000
8a	Taxable interest income. Attach Schedule B if over $400	8100
8b	Tax-exempt interest income (don't include on line 8a)	1900
9	Dividend income. Attach Schedule B if over $400	
10	Taxable refunds, credits, or offsets of state and local income taxes	
11	Alimony received	
12	Business income or (loss). Attach Schedule C or C-EZ	
13	Capital gain or (loss). Attach Schedule D	
14	Capital gain distributions not reported on line 13	
15	Other gains or (losses). Attach Form 4797	
16a	Total IRA distributions	
16b	Taxable amount	400
17a	Total pensions and annuities: 800	
17b	Taxable amount	57114
18	Rents, royalties, partnerships, estates, trusts, etc. Attach Schedule E	
19	Farm income or (loss). Attach Schedule F	
20	Unemployment compensation	
21a	Social security benefits	
21b	Taxable amount	
22	Other income	
23	**Total income**	115614

Adjustments to Income

24a	Your IRA deduction	2000
24b	Spouse's IRA deduction	
25	One-half of self-employment tax	
26	Self-employed health insurance deduction	
27	Keogh retirement plan and self-employed SEP deduction	
28	Penalty on early withdrawal of savings	
29	Alimony paid	
30	**Total adjustments**	2000

Adjusted Gross Income
31. Subtract line 30 from line 23. This is your **adjusted gross income**: **113614**

Cat. No. 12598V   Form **1040** (1992)

Chapter 8

Exhibit 8.2 Form 1040–U.S. Individual Income Tax Return

Form 1040 (1992) — Page 2

Tax Computation (See page 22.)	32 Amount from line 31 (adjusted gross income)	32	113614
	33a Check if: ☐ You were 65 or older, ☐ Blind; ☐ Spouse was 65 or older, ☐ Blind. Add the number of boxes checked above and enter the total here ▶ 33a		
	b If your parent (or someone else) can claim you as a dependent, check here ▶ 33b ☐		
	c If you are married filing separately and your spouse itemizes deductions or you are a dual-status alien, see page 22 and check here ▶ 33c ☐		
	34 Enter the larger of your: Itemized deductions from Schedule A, line 26, OR Standard deduction shown below for your filing status. But if you checked any box on line 33a or b, go to page 22 to find your standard deduction. If you checked box 33c, your standard deduction is zero. • Single—$3,600 • Head of household—$5,250 • Married filing jointly or Qualifying widow(er)—$6,000 • Married filing separately—$3,000	34	8000
	35 Subtract line 34 from line 32	35	105614
	36 If line 32 is $78,950 or less, multiply $2,300 by the total number of exemptions claimed on line 6e. If line 32 is over $78,950, see the worksheet on page 23 for the amount to enter	36	2300
If you want the IRS to figure your tax, see page 23.	37 **Taxable income.** Subtract line 36 from line 35. If line 36 is more than line 35, enter -0-	37	103314
	38 Enter tax. Check if from a ☐ Tax Table, b ☒ Tax Rate Schedules, c ☐ Schedule D, or d ☐ Form 8615 (see page 23). Amount, if any, from Form(s) 8814 ▶ e _____	38	28400
	39 Additional taxes (see page 23). Check if from a ☐ Form 4970 b ☐ Form 4972	39	
	40 Add lines 38 and 39 ▶	40	28400
Credits (See page 23.)	41 Credit for child and dependent care expenses. Attach Form 2441	41	
	42 Credit for the elderly or the disabled. Attach Schedule R	42	
	43 Foreign tax credit. Attach Form 1116	43	
	44 Other credits (see page 24). Check if from a ☐ Form 3800 b ☐ Form 8396 c ☐ Form 8801 d ☐ Form (specify)	44	
	45 Add lines 41 through 44	45	
	46 Subtract line 45 from line 40. If line 45 is more than line 40, enter -0- ▶	46	28400
Other Taxes	47 Self-employment tax. Attach Schedule SE. Also, see line 25	47	
	48 Alternative minimum tax. Attach Form 6251	48	
	49 Recapture taxes (see page 25). Check if from ☐ Form 4255 b ☐ Form 8611 c ☐ Form 8828	49	
	50 Social security and Medicare tax on tip income not reported to employer. Attach Form 4137	50	
	51 Tax on qualified retirement plans, including IRAs. Attach Form 5329	51	
	52 Advance earned income credit payments from Form W-2	52	
	53 Add lines 46 through 52. This is your **total tax** ▶	53	28400
Payments Attach Forms W-2, W-2G, and 1099-R on the front.	54 Federal income tax withheld. If any is from Form(s) 1099, check ▶ ☐	54	28401
	55 1992 estimated tax payments and amount applied from 1991 return	55	
	56 **Earned income credit.** Attach Schedule EIC	56	
	57 Amount paid with Form 4868 (extension request)	57	
	58 Excess social security, Medicare, and RRTA tax withheld (see page 26)	58	
	59 Other payments (see page 26). Check if from a ☐ Form 2439 b ☐ Form 4136	59	
	60 Add lines 54 through 59. These are your **total payments** ▶	60	28401
Refund or Amount You Owe Attach check or money order on top of Form(s) W-2, etc., on the front.	61 If line 60 is more than line 53, subtract line 53 from line 60. This is the amount you **OVERPAID** ▶	61	1
	62 Amount of line 61 you want **REFUNDED TO YOU** ▶	62	1
	63 Amount of line 61 you want **APPLIED TO YOUR 1993 ESTIMATED TAX** ▶ 63		
	64 If line 53 is more than line 60, subtract line 60 from line 53. This is the **AMOUNT YOU OWE**. Attach check or money order for full amount payable to "Internal Revenue Service." Write your name, address, social security number, daytime phone number, and "1992 Form 1040" on it	64	
	65 Estimated tax penalty (see page 27). Also include on line 64	65	

Sign Here
Keep a copy of this return for your records.

Under penalties of perjury, I declare that I have examined this return and accompanying schedules and statements, and to the best of my knowledge and belief, they are true, correct, and complete. Declaration of preparer (other than taxpayer) is based on all information of which preparer has any knowledge.

Your signature ▶ *Charles C. Smith*   Date 4-15-93   Your occupation CHOCOLATE MAKER
Spouse's signature. If a joint return, BOTH must sign.   Date   Spouse's occupation

Paid Preparer's Use Only
Preparer's signature ▶ *Ryan Jones*   Date 4-15-93   Check if self-employed ☒   Preparer's social security no. 000:00:0000
Firm's name (or yours if self-employed) and address ▶ RYAN JONES 1313 TAX ST. CANDYLAND, IL   E.I. No. 00   ZIP code 00000

☆ U.S. GOVERNMENT PRINTING OFFICE: 1992 315-034

84

Personal Cash Flow Analysis

Exhibit 8.3 Schedule A–Itemized Deductions

SCHEDULES A&B (Form 1040)
Department of the Treasury
Internal Revenue Service (B)

Schedule A—Itemized Deductions
(Schedule B is on back)
▶ Attach to Form 1040. ▶ See Instructions for Schedules A and B (Form 1040).

OMB No. 1545-0074
1992
Attachment Sequence No. 07

Name(s) shown on Form 1040: **CHARLES C. SMITH**
Your social security number: 000 00 0000

Medical and Dental Expenses		Caution: Do not include expenses reimbursed or paid by others.	
	1	Medical and dental expenses (see page A-1)	
	2	Enter amount from Form 1040, line 32	
	3	Multiply line 2 above by 7.5% (.075)	
	4	Subtract line 3 from line 1. If zero or less, enter -0- ▶	
Taxes You Paid (See page A-1.)	5	State and local income taxes	
	6	Real estate taxes (see page A-2)	
	7	Other taxes. List—include personal property taxes ▶	
	8	Add lines 5 through 7 ▶	
Interest You Paid (See page A-2.) Note: Personal interest is not deductible.	9a	Home mortgage interest and points reported to you on Form 1098	8000
	b	Home mortgage interest not reported to you on Form 1098. If paid to an individual, show that person's name and address. ▶	
	10	Points not reported to you on Form 1098. See page A-3 for special rules	
	11	Investment interest. If required, attach Form 4952. (See page A-3.)	
	12	Add lines 9a through 11 ▶	8000
Gifts to Charity (See page A-3.)		Caution: If you made a charitable contribution and received a benefit in return, see page A-3.	
	13	Contributions by cash or check	
	14	Other than by cash or check. If over $500, you **MUST** attach Form 8283	
	15	Carryover from prior year	
	16	Add lines 13 through 15 ▶	
Casualty and Theft Losses	17	Casualty or theft loss(es). Attach Form 4684. (See page A-4.) ▶	
Moving Expenses	18	Moving expenses. Attach Form 3903 or 3903F. (See page A-4.) ▶	
Job Expenses and Most Other Miscellaneous Deductions (See page A-5 for expenses to deduct here.)	19	Unreimbursed employee expenses—job travel, union dues, job education, etc. If required, you **MUST** attach Form 2106. (See page A-4.) ▶	
	20	Other expenses—investment, tax preparation, safe deposit box, etc. List type and amount ▶	
	21	Add lines 19 and 20	
	22	Enter amount from Form 1040, line 32	
	23	Multiply line 22 above by 2% (.02)	
	24	Subtract line 23 from line 21. If zero or less, enter -0- ▶	
Other Miscellaneous Deductions	25	Other—from list on page A-5. List type and amount ▶	
Total Itemized Deductions	26	Is the amount on Form 1040, line 32, more than $105,250 (more than $52,625 if married filing separately)? • **NO.** Your deduction is not limited. Add lines 4, 8, 12, 16, 17, 18, 24, and 25. • **YES.** Your deduction may be limited. See page A-5 for the amount to enter. Caution: Be sure to enter on Form 1040, line 34, the **LARGER** of the amount on line 26 above or your standard deduction.	8000

For Paperwork Reduction Act Notice, see Form 1040 instructions. Cat. No. 12611D Schedule A (Form 1040) 1992

Chapter 8

Exhibit 8.4 Schedule B—Interest and Dividend Income

Schedules A&B (Form 1040) 1992
OMB No. 1545-0074 Page **2**

Name(s) shown on Form 1040. Do not enter name and social security number if shown on other side. Your social security number

Schedule B—Interest and Dividend Income
Attachment Sequence No. **08**

Part I Interest Income
(See pages 14 and B-1.)

If you had over $400 in taxable interest income OR are claiming the exclusion of interest from series EE U.S. savings bonds issued after 1989, you must complete this part. List ALL interest you received. If you had over $400 in taxable interest income, you must also complete Part III. If you received, as a nominee, interest that actually belongs to another person, or you received or paid accrued interest on securities transferred between interest payment dates, see page B-1.

Note: If you received a Form 1099-INT, Form 1099-OID, or substitute statement from a brokerage firm, list the firm's name as the payer and enter the total interest shown on that form.

	Interest Income		Amount
1	List name of payer—if any interest income is from seller-financed mortgages, see page B-1 and list this interest first ▶ CHARLIE'S CHOCOLATE COMPANY		7500
	FIRST BANK	1	600
2	Add the amounts on line 1	2	8100
3	Excludable interest on series EE U.S. savings bonds issued after 1989 from Form 8815, line 14. You MUST attach Form 8815 to Form 1040	3	
4	Subtract line 3 from line 2. Enter the result here and on Form 1040, line 8a ▶	4	8100

Part II Dividend Income
(See pages 15 and B-1.)

If you had over $400 in gross dividends and/or other distributions on stock, you must complete this part and Part III. If you received, as a nominee, dividends that actually belong to another person, see page B-1.

Note: If you received a Form 1099-DIV or substitute statement from a brokerage firm, list the firm's name as the payer and enter the total dividends shown on that form.

	Dividend Income		Amount
5	List name of payer—include on this line capital gain distributions, nontaxable distributions, etc. ▶	5	
6	Add the amounts on line 5	6	
7	Capital gain distributions. Enter here and on Schedule D*	7	
8	Nontaxable distributions. (See the inst. for Form 1040, line 9.)	8	
9	Add lines 7 and 8	9	
10	Subtract line 9 from line 6. Enter the result here and on Form 1040, line 9 ▶	10	

*If you received capital gain distributions but do not need Schedule D to report any other gains or losses, see the instructions for Form 1040, lines 13 and 14.

Part III Foreign Accounts and Foreign Trusts
(See page B-2.)

If you had over $400 of interest or dividends OR had a foreign account or were a grantor of, or a transferor to, a foreign trust, you must complete this part.

		Yes	No
11a	At any time during 1992, did you have an interest in or a signature or other authority over a financial account in a foreign country, such as a bank account, securities account, or other financial account? See page B-2 for exceptions and filing requirements for Form TD F 90-22.1		
b	If "Yes," enter the name of the foreign country ▶		
12	Were you the grantor of, or transferor to, a foreign trust that existed during 1992, whether or not you have any beneficial interest in it? If "Yes," you may have to file Form 3520, 3520-A, or 926		

For Paperwork Reduction Act Notice, see Form 1040 instructions. Schedule B (Form 1040) 1992

☆ U.S. GOVERNMENT PRINTING OFFICE: 1992 315-034

Personal Cash Flow Analysis

Exhibit 8.5 Supplemental Income and Loss

SCHEDULE E (Form 1040)
Department of the Treasury
Internal Revenue Service (X)

Supplemental Income and Loss
(From rental real estate, royalties, partnerships, estates, trusts, REMICs, etc.)
► Attach to Form 1040 or Form 1041.
► See Instructions for Schedule E (Form 1040).

OMB No. 1545-0074
1992
Attachment Sequence No. 13

Name(s) shown on return: **CHARLES C. SMITH**
Your social security number: **000 00 0000**

Part I — Income or Loss From Rental Real Estate and Royalties
Note: Report income and expenses from the rental of personal property on Schedule C or C-EZ. Report farm rental income or loss from Form 4835 on page 2, line 39.

1 Show the kind and location of each rental real estate property:
- A. CHARLIE'S CHOC. COMP. OPER. FACILITY, 1000 E. DEBRA
- B. RENTAL PROPERTY, 50 N. SHORE
- C.

2 For each rental real estate property listed on line 1, did you or your family use it for personal purposes for more than the greater of 14 days or 10% of the total days rented at fair rental value during the tax year? (See page E-1.)
- A. No (X)
- B. No (X)
- C.

		Properties A	Properties B	Properties C	Totals (Add columns A, B, and C)
Income:					
3	Rents received	100000	14400		3 114400
4	Royalties received				4
Expenses:					
5	Advertising				
6	Auto and travel (see page E-2)				
7	Cleaning and maintenance				
8	Commissions				
9	Insurance		350		
10	Legal and other professional fees				
11	Management fees				
12	Mortgage interest paid to banks, etc. (see page E-2)	46000	5200		12 51200
13	Other interest				
14	Repairs		500		
15	Supplies				
16	Taxes		2400		
17	Utilities				
18	Other (list) ►				
19	Add lines 5 through 18	46000	8450		19 54450
20	Depreciation expense or depletion (see page E-2)	22200	3636		20 25836
21	Total expenses. Add lines 19 and 20	68200	12086		
22	Income or (loss) from rental real estate or royalty properties. Subtract line 21 from line 3 (rents) or line 4 (royalties). If the result is a (loss), see page E-2 to find out if you must file Form 6198	31800	2314		
23	Deductible rental real estate loss. Caution: Your rental real estate loss on line 22 may be limited. See page E-3 to find out if you must file Form 8582	( )	( )	( )	

24 Income. Add positive amounts shown on line 22. **Do not** include any losses 24 34114

25 Losses. Add royalty losses from line 22 and rental real estate losses from line 23. Enter the total losses here .... 25 (   )

26 Total rental real estate and royalty income or (loss). Combine lines 24 and 25. Enter the result here. If Parts II, III, IV, and line 39 on page 2 do not apply to you, also enter this amount on Form 1040, line 18. Otherwise, include this amount in the total on line 40 on page 2 .... 26 34114

For Paperwork Reduction Act Notice, see Form 1040 instructions. Cat. No. 11344L Schedule E (Form 1040) 1992

43

87

Chapter 8

Exhibit 8.6 Supplemental Income and Loss

Schedule E (Form 1040) 1992 — Attachment Sequence No. 13 — Page 2

Name(s) shown on return. Do not enter name and social security number if shown on other side. — Your social security number

Note: *If you report amounts from farming or fishing on Schedule E, you must enter your gross income from those activities on line 41 below.*

Part II Income or Loss From Partnerships and S Corporations

If you report a loss from an at-risk activity, you MUST check either column (e) or (f) of line 27 to describe your investment in the activity. See page E-3. If you check column (f), you must attach **Form 6198**.

27	(a) Name	(b) Enter P for partnership; S for S corporation	(c) Check if foreign partnership	(d) Employer identification number	Investment At Risk? (e) All is at risk / (f) Some is not at risk
A	CHARLIE'S CHOCOLATE COMPANY	S		00000 0000	X
B					
C					
D					
E					

	Passive Income and Loss		Nonpassive Income and Loss		
	(g) Passive loss allowed (attach Form 8582 if required)	(h) Passive income from Schedule K-1	(i) Nonpassive loss from Schedule K-1	(j) Section 179 expense deduction from Form 4562	(k) Nonpassive income from Schedule K-1
A					23000
B					
C					
D					
E					

28a Totals					23000
b Totals					

29 Add columns (h) and (k) of line 28a 29 23000
30 Add columns (g), (i), and (j) of line 28b . . . . 30 (   )
31 Total partnership and S corporation income or (loss). Combine lines 29 and 30. Enter the result here and include in the total on line 40 below 31 23000

Part III Income or Loss From Estates and Trusts

32	(a) Name	(b) Employer identification number
A		
B		
C		

	Passive Income and Loss		Nonpassive Income and Loss	
	(c) Passive deduction or loss allowed (attach Form 8582 if required)	(d) Passive income from Schedule K-1	(e) Deduction or loss from Schedule K-1	(f) Other income from Schedule K-1
A				
B				
C				

33a Totals				
b Totals				

34 Add columns (d) and (f) of line 33a 34
35 Add columns (c) and (e) of line 33b . . . . 35 (   )
36 Total estate and trust income or (loss). Combine lines 34 and 35. Enter the result here and include in the total on line 40 below 36

Part IV Income or Loss From Real Estate Mortgage Investment Conduits (REMICs)—Residual Holder

37	(a) Name	(b) Employer identification number	(c) Excess inclusion from Schedules Q, line 2c (see page E-4)	(d) Taxable income (net loss) from Schedules Q, line 1b	(e) Income from Schedules Q, line 3b

38 Combine columns (d) and (e) only. Enter the result here and include in the total on line 40 below 38

Part V Summary

39 Net farm rental income or (loss) from **Form 4835**. Also, complete line 41 below 39
40 TOTAL income or (loss). Combine lines 26, 31, 36, 38, and 39. Enter the result here and on Form 1040, line 18 . . . . ▶ 40 57114
41 **Reconciliation of Farming and Fishing Income:** Enter your gross farming and fishing income reported in Parts II and III and on line 39 (see page E-4) 41

88

Personal Cash Flow Analysis

ing non-taxable incomes) are included in the cash available calculation.

To **exclude** them, simply **subtract the b line.**

8. Other gains/losses (line 15) are included in cash available if they arise through normal business operation. To **include** them, make **no adjustment.**

   Other gains/losses frequently consist, however, of sales of business property, which are one-time events. If this is the case, **subtract the amount on line 15** to **exclude** them.

9. Capital gains/losses (lines 13 and 14) are tricky. To **exclude** these, **subtract** the amount on line 13 or 14. If you are including them, be sure to only include actual cash flows which occurred within the years that you are analyzing.

10. Alimony received (line 11) can be included if it is expected to continue. To **include** it, make **no adjustment**.

    If it is **not** to be included, then it should be **subtracted**.

11. Taxable refunds, credits, or offsets of state and local income taxes (line 10) should **always be subtracted**. These are cash expenses, which are non-taxable.

12. Dividend and interest income (lines 9 and 8a) can be included if there is a history and if the income is expected to continue. (Be sure to check if the individual still owns the asset producing the income). To **include** these cash flows, **make no adjustment**.

    If the conditions are not met, and you do **not** want to include the income, then **subtract** the amount which is not expected to continue. Also, note that you should

Chapter 8

subtract any zero-coupon bond interest and any dividends which are reinvested since these incomes do not represent actual cash flows.

13. Tax-exempt interest income (line 8b) can be included if it is expected to continue. To **include** this as cash available, the amount must be **added** back since it is non-taxable income.

    To **exclude** this income, make **no adjustment**. (Be sure to exclude zero-coupon bond interest.)

14. Look for a **Form 2106** (Employee Business Expenses). **Subtract** all **cash** expenses found on this form. (Note that when using the standard deduction for auto mileage, 11 cents of the 28 cents per mile is depreciation.)

15. Subtract the **total tax** (line 53).

When all of the above adjustments have been made, the sum will be the **"TOTAL AVAILABLE."** Also sum the **"TOTAL DEBT SERVICE"** (both interest and principal payments on all personal debts to be made for the next 12 months).

Next, calculate a **"DEBT TO INCOME"** ratio by taking each period's **TOTAL DEBT SERVICE** divided by the **TOTAL AVAILABLE**. It is also helpful to list the **"EXCESS"** or **"DEFICIT"** coverage which is the difference between the **TOTAL AVAILABLE** and the **TOTAL DEBT SERVICE**. Finally, it may also be appropriate to calculate a **"DEBT SERVICE COVERAGE RATIO"** by taking each period's **TOTAL AVAILABLE** divided by the **TOTAL DEBT SERVICE**.

Personal Cash Flow Analysis

DETAILED EXPLANATION

Start with total income (line 23 of Form 1040). **Enter $115,614.** Notice the IRA deduction on line 24a. Mr. Smith earned $2,000 which was deducted from total income for tax purposes only. Such funds could be used for debt service in the future; therefore, **no adjustment is made for the IRA deduction**.

The $57,114 figure on line 18 should be analyzed by examining Schedule E. First examine the two properties on page one of Schedule E. Property A is the operating facility for Charlie's Chocolate Company. Since this property is included in the company cash flow analysis, it should be **excluded** from the personal cash flow analysis. Property B is a rental property owned by Mr. Smith which does not affect the company operations. Property B should be **included** in the personal cash flow analysis. To exclude property A and to include property B perform the following steps:

1. Subtract line 26 of Schedule E. Subtract $34,114.
2. Subtract line 19 of Schedule E for property B only. Subtract $8,450.
3. Add line 12 of Schedule E for property B. Add $5,200.
4. Add line 3 of Schedule E for property B. Add $14,400.

Next, turn to page two of Schedule E. The $23,000 figure on line 31 represents the net income of Charlie's Chocolate Company. This income is "passed through" to Mr. Smith for tax purposes; however, it does not represent personal cash flow. These monies were included in the company cash flow analysis. **Subtract $23,000.** We know, however, that the

Chapter 8

company distributed $5,000 to Mr. Smith in 1992. This distribution was subtracted from the company cash available. It can be added to personal cash flow since it represents an actual payment to Mr. Smith. **Add $5,000.**

Examine line 17 of Form 1040. Mr. Smith receives $800 annually from an annuity; however, only $400 of this income is taxable. The income is assumed to be normal and ongoing, so it should be included in cash available. **Subtract the b line, and add back the a line. Subtract $400, and add back $800**.

Mr. Smith's interest income on line 8a is assumed to be normal and ongoing, so it should be included in cash available. **To include interest income, make no adjustment.**

Mr. Smith also earned tax exempt interest income of $1,900 in 1992. The amount on line 8b does represent actual cash available to Mr. Smith, even though it is not taxable. The income is assumed to be normal and ongoing, so **add $1,900.**

'Subtract the total tax (line 53). Subtract $28,400.

PERSONAL CASH FLOW CALCULATION

A summary of the above described calculation is as follows:

Total income (line 23)	$ 115,614
Less: property income (Sched. E, line 36)	($ 34,114)
Less: cash prop. exp. (Sched. E, line 19)	($ 8,450)
Add: property interest (Sched. E, line 12)	$ 5,200
Add: property income (Sched. E, line 3)	$ 14,400
Less: company income (Sched. E, line 31)	($ 23,000)
Add: dividend from company	$ 5,000
Less: taxable pension income (line 17b)	($ 400)
Add: actual pension income (line 17a)	$ 800
Add: tax-exempt interest (line 8b)	$ 1,900
Less: total tax (line 53)	$ 28,400)
TOTAL PERSONAL CASH AVAILABLE	$ 48,550

Personal Cash Flow Analysis

Next calculate the **TOTAL DEBT SERVICE:**

Annual Payment	Loan:	Description of payment:
$ 8,600	$50,000 Mortgage	Monthly principal payments of $833 plus accrued interest at 8%.
$ 2,712	$5,000 Auto Loan	Monthly principal and interest payments of $226.
$10,032	$100,000 Mortgage	Monthly principal and interest payments of $836.
$21,344	**TOTAL DEBT SERVICE REQUIRED ANNUALLY**	

The **DEBT TO INCOME** equals **TOTAL DEBT SERVICE** divided by **TOTAL AVAILABLE:**

TOTAL DEBT SERVICE	$21,344
TOTAL CASH AVAILABLE	$48,550
DEBT TO INCOME	**44.0%**

PERSONAL CASH FLOW ANALYSIS

The debt to income ratio of 44 percent is relatively high. Total annual debt service should generally not exceed 35 to 45 percent of annual cash available. However, in this particular case, the $27,000 excess cash flow over debt service is most likely sufficient to pay Mr. Smith's living expenses and to provide an extra cushion, if necessary. Mr. Smith's standard of living should, however, also be examined to verify that the excess is, indeed, sufficient.

Chapter 9

LOAN STRUCTURING AND DEFINITIONS

COMMERCIAL LOAN FACILITIES

The following list represents five general types of loan facilities that banks offer:

1. A **single-payment note** is a loan whereby the entire principal and interest amount is due in one payment at the maturity date.
2. A **line of credit** is a facility allowing the borrower to draw and repay funds up to a specified amount at his or her discretion.
3. A **letter of credit** is a commitment allowing a third party to draw funds for which the borrower is liable. For example, a real estate developer will typically have letters of credit "in favor of" (or payable to) municipalities. The municipalities have the right to draw the funds if the borrower does not fulfill his or her duties to develop

Chapter 9

the land. If the municipality draws the funds, the developer is responsible for repaying the bank.

4. A **commercial real estate mortgage** is a loan secured by real estate which is repaid by a regular principal and interest payment or by a regular principal payment plus accrued interest.

5. A **commercial installment note or term loan** is a loan other than a mortgage with some type of regular payment.

COMMERCIAL LOAN TYPES/REASONS FOR BORROWING

The following list of loan types represents the four reasons for commercial borrowing:

1. Bridge Loans[3] bridge a gap until a specific event occurs which allows the loan to be repaid. Bridge loans can be repaid from three different sources:

    a. The sale of non-current assets

    b. Refinancing debt with debt

    c. The infusion of equity

2. Seasonal Loans[3] are short-term facilities typically used to fund inventory build-ups or expenses. An example of a seasonal loan is a line of credit extended to a retailer to fund purchases of Christmas products. The line is extended as inventory increases before Christmas. As inventory is sold, it converts to receivables and eventually

---

3 Morsman, Edgar M., Jr. "Commercial Loan Sructuring." *The Journal of Commercial Bank Lending.* Copyright 1991 by Robert Morris Associates. Reprinted with permission from *The Journal of Commercial Lending,* November 1991. pp. 25–38.

Loan Structuring and Definitions

to cash. During this conversion, the bank is repaid. Seasonal loan analysis focuses on the balance sheet (as inventory converts to receivables and then to cash). In fact, a seasonal loan can be repaid even if the borrower is not profitable. Such a line of credit would typically be secured by receivables, inventory, and equipment.

3. Term Loans[3] are long-term facilities repaid from income generated by the business. Term loans are frequently used to purchase fixed assets or to finance a change of ownership or an acquisition. Sufficient net incomes and future profit potential are important criteria for approving term loans. Term loan facilities typically consist of commercial mortgages secured by real estate or commercial installment loans secured by equipment.

4. Permanent Working Capital Loans[3] are revolving credit facilities used to purchase current assets or to pay current liabilities. This type of lending is referred to as "permanent working capital lending" because it is really a substitute for owners' equity. It is also referred to as "asset-based lending" because the amount of funds that the bank is willing to lend at any given time is based on the level of assets the borrower provides for collateral; typically, accounts receivable and inventory are used for security. Working capital loans are even referred to as "evergreen loans" since, unlike seasonal loans, these loans are rarely paid down to a low amount at any time during the year. They should, therefore, be restricted to growing and profitable businesses whose long-term performance is highly likely.

Chapter 9

LOAN TERM AND AMORTIZATION

A loan's **term, maturity, expiration, or balloon** refers to its duration or to the time at which the loan commitment ends. The remaining principal and all accrued interest are due at this time. Upon maturity, the loan is typically reviewed by both the bank and the borrower. Either party may decide not to renew the loan after it has expired.

A loan's **amortization** is the length of time over which its payments are spread. The amortization may differ from the term; in fact, the amortization is typically a longer period of time than the term for a commercial installment or mortgage loan. Note the two types of loan amortization:

1. The regular **principal and interest** payment is fixed over the life of the loan (for example, conventional residential mortgages and auto loans almost always use this method).

2. Only the principal payment amount is fixed. Accrued interest on the principal balance is usually due along with the regular principal payment. The total **principal plus interest** payment on this type of loan decreases each period as the principal balance decreases.

LOAN PRICING

Interest rates can be structured along the following continuum:

1. Fixed for the term of the loan

2. Fixed with periodic adjustments tied to an index such as a publicly documented prime rate or U.S. Treasury yields

3. Fixed or variable with a **floor** (minimum rate) and/or a **ceiling** (maximum rate)

Loan Structuring and Definitions

4. Variable according to the bank's own reference rate

Points are fees paid up front for a loan commitment. One point is equal to one percent of the loan commitment.

Pre-payment penalties can vary along the following continuum:

1. A penalty is assessed if the borrower repays the debt during the term of the loan.
2. A penalty is assessed if the borrower repays the debt by any means other than the internally generated cash flows of the company. (This would include a refinance at your own bank.)
3. A penalty is assessed only if the borrower repays the debt through refinance with another institution.

COLLATERAL

1. First mortgage: Mortgages are the vehicles by which the bank takes real estate as collateral. The first mortgage holder has the first right (before the second mortgage holder and before any other creditors) of repayment from funds gained through liquidation of the asset.
2. Second mortgage: The second mortgage holder has the right of repayment through liquidation after the first mortgage holder has been repaid. A second mortgage holder may force liquidation of collateral, but it must pay the first mortgage holder in full before receiving any funds.
3. Assignment of Beneficial Interests (ABI): This frequently occurs when a property is held in a trust. To hold it as collateral, the bank has the interests of the trust assigned to it.

Chapter 9

4. Assignment of Rents: This allows rent payments from tenants to be paid directly to the bank if the borrower defaults on a mortgage or if the bank takes ownership or control of the property.

5. Assignment of any other future source of income: In addition to rent or lease streams, any present or future source of cash can be specifically assigned to the bank. This includes payments on accounts or notes receivable, tax refunds, insurance refunds, life insurance proceeds, or lottery winnings. Note that some income streams cannot, by law, be assigned. For example, workman's compensation and FCC licenses to broadcasters are not assignable.

6. Business Assets: The borrower can assign business assets to the bank for collateral. This is accomplished when the borrower 1) signs a "Security Agreement" with the bank, and 2) the bank registers a "UCC filing" with the state or county government. A "General Business Security Agreement" (GBSA) or a "UCC Blanket Lien" refers to an assignment of **all** business assets to the bank.

    Business Assets can include accounts receivable, fixed assets, and inventory. Business assets exclude real estate (land, buildings, and all attached fixtures) which requires a mortgage to be held as collateral. Business assets also exclude inventory when suppliers of the inventory have a specific lien on that inventory until it is paid for. Finally, in Illinois, business assets do not include vehicles since liens must be taken by the title of each collateral vehicle.

7. Cross-Collateralization: This is an agreement whereby two or more separate loans become secured by the collateral of the other loan or loans (in addition to being secured by their own collateral).

Loan Structuring and Definitions

8. Loan to Value Ratio: The loan to value ratio is the ratio of one or more loan balances (or loan commitments) divided by the value of the collateral of the loan(s).

   When calculating the loan to value or the loan to liquidation value for a line of credit, the proper **loan** amount to consider is the total amount that could be drawn on the line today. If there is an advance formula, then the maximum amount drawable on the line can be determined by the advance formula.

Exhibit 9.1 illustrates the loan to value and loan to liquidation value for a commercial mortgage.

9. Loan to Liquidation Value Ratio: The loan to liquidation value is the ratio of the loan balances (or commitments) divided by the liquidation or discounted value of the collateral.

   This ratio is useful when one type of collateral, such as inventory, is discounted by 50 percent to determine a liquidation value, while another type of collateral for the same loan such as receivables is discounted by 25 per-

Exhibit 9.1

Commercial Mortgage Balance	$ 50,000
Appraised Value of Collateral Property	$100,000
Liquidation Value (75% of Appraised Value)	$ 75,000

Loan to Value	50%
Loan to Liquidation Value	67%

Chapter 9

cent. You can first discount all collateral and then calculate a liquidation ratio. This ratio is also necessary when analyzing a second mortgage. First, discount the value of the property by the appropriate percentage, and **then** subtract the first mortgage balance to leave a liquidation value.

10. Life Cycle Value of Inventory: Inventory holds different values to the bank as collateral throughout its life. Raw materials can usually be sold back to suppliers or to other companies in liquidation. Since they are relatively marketable, raw materials do have value to the bank as collateral. Work in process is generally not marketable, so it is usually not considered for advance formulas or loan to value ratios. Finally, finished goods can generally be liquidated, so they do have value to the bank.

11. Negative Asset Pledge: This is a contract whereby the borrower agrees not to pledge a certain asset as collateral to anyone else. This ensures that, although the bank has not taken the asset as collateral, the asset would be available for liquidation in the event of default. (In addition, a bank holding a first mortgage may contractually limit the ability of the borrower to pledge the property for a second mortgage.)

GUARANTEES

A guarantee occurs when a third party agrees to repay debt if the borrower defaults. For example, company owners are frequently required by the bank to personally guarantee repayment of loans made to the company. In addition, corporations frequently guarantee loans made to company owners or to related companies. Guarantees can be:

Loan Structuring and Definitions

1. Unsecured or Secured: A secured guarantee occurs when the guarantor pledges some personal asset as collateral along with his or her guarantee. Asset pledges by guarantors frequently include residential mortgages, mortgages on company operating facilities, or stock of the borrowing company.

2. Unconditional or Conditional: A conditional guarantee follows some pre-specified condition such as a requirement that collateral must be liquidated before a guarantee can be enforced.

3. Unlimited or Limited: A limited guarantee could, for example, limit a guarantor's personal liability to his pro rata share of ownership of the company.

SUBORDINATION REQUIREMENTS

Subordination occurs when debt (for example, an officer debt to the company) is placed in the "second position." This means that the subordinated debt cannot be repaid in the event of liquidation until the senior debt (for example, bank debt in the "first position") is repaid. Such agreements are usually made in conjunction with a subordinated debt repayment restriction.

DEBT REPAYMENT RESTRICTIONS

Restrictions on the repayment of debts (usually debt to officers) are frequently made in conjunction with subordination to ensure that the bank debts would be repaid before other debts. Restrictions could be made according to the following continuum:

1. No repayment of principal or interest is allowed.
2. No repayment of principal may be made, but interest payments are allowed.
3. Repayment of a specific periodic principal payment is allowed along with interest payments.
4. Repayment of any principal and interest payments are allowed as long as some other requirement is followed. Other requirements could include keeping the bank debt repayment current or showing evidence of a certain debt service coverage ratio or maintaining minimum liquidity or leverage ratios.

OTHER REQUIREMENTS

Advance formulas are mathematical formulas which determine the amount of funds the bank will lend. For example, at any one time, the bank may be willing to lend up to 75 percent of "eligible" accounts receivable less than 90 days plus 50 percent of inventory, less work in process.

"Eligible" accounts receivable typically exclude all receivables of any customer who has 10 percent or more of his total balance in the over 90 days category. "Eligible" receivables also typically exclude all receivables of any customer whose receivables represent 10 percent or more of the total accounts receivable balance.

Clean-up periods are period of time where the borrower must maintain a zero loan balance. The bank will typically require a 60-day clean-up period annually on a line of credit.

Cross-defaults occur when default on one loan constitutes default on other loans (this can include both loans at one bank or loans at several banks).

Chapter 10

SAMPLE LOAN PRESENTATION

The following loan presentation typifies the format and the analytical orientation of a written proposal presented to a bank loan committee for approval.

MEMORANDUM

March 1, 1994

To: Officers Loan Committee
Fr: Ken Pirok
Credit Analyst
Re: Loan request for Charlie's Chocolate Company, Inc.

APPLICANT   PRINCIPAL(S)   POSITION   OWNERSHIP

Charlie's Chocolate
Company, Inc.   Charles Smith   President   100%

Chapter 10

LOAN REQUEST:	RENEWAL/INCREASE—$150,000 LINE OF CREDIT
PURPOSE:	To renew the existing $100,000 short-term working capital line of credit and to increase the commitment due to rapid growth
PRICING:	8.0%, fixed / $1,500 fee
REPAYMENT TERMS:	One year term / Interest only payments required monthly
COLLATERAL:	All business assets via blanket security agreement
OTHER SUPPORT:	The unlimited, unsecured personal guarantee of Mr. Charles Smith
ADVANCE FORMULA:	Advances will be limited to 75 percent of accounts receivable less than 90 days plus 50 percent of inventory less work in process.
CONDITIONS OF APPROVAL:	Annual receipt of CPA prepared, company financial statements, personal financial statement, and personal tax returns
PROPOSED TOTAL BANK COMMITMENT:	$1,093,000

BACKGROUND

Charlie's Chocolate Company, Incorporated is a manufacturer and wholesaler of fine chocolates and other chocolate products. The company's chocolates are sold

Sample Loan Presentation

primarily to candy stores and gift shops throughout the Midwest.

Mr. Charles Smith started the company in late 1990 by purchasing the equipment of a failing chocolate manufacturer. The company was incorporated as an Illinois Subchapter S corporation at that time.

Mr. Smith owns 100 percent of the common stock of the company. He has also made a $75,000 loan to the company. Currently, the company pays interest each month on this loan to Mr. Smith at an annual rate of 10.0 percent. The principal on the loan is not currently being repaid, and the loan is subordinate to all other debt per an agreement with the bank.

Mr. Smith also owns the building in which the company operates. He owns this building personally and rents it to the company. The company rents on a triple net basis.

The company financial statements are compiled by Ryan Jones, CPA. The company SIC code is 2064.

LOAN RELATIONSHIP

Charlie's Chocolate Company:

Current Balance	Current Maturity	Monthly Payment	Interest Rate	Comments
$100,000	3-15-94	Interest	8.0%	Working Capital
$230,000	3-15-95	$2,500 plus int.	8.0%	Company Purchase
$ 58,000	3-15-95	$1,657 P&I	8.0%	Equipment Purchase
$500,000	3-15-97	$4,167 P&I	8.0%	Operating Facility
$ 50,000	3-15-97	$ 833 plus int.	8.0%	Rental Property
$ 5,000	6-21-96	$ 226 P&I	8.0%	Auto Loan
$100,000	2-25-94	$ 836 P&I	8.0%	Personal Residence

Chapter 10

BUSINESS PLAN / MANAGEMENT

The stated mission of the company is, "to provide a complete line of fine chocolates for true chocolate lovers." The company's geographic market is the entire-midwest, and their "complete line" of chocolates now includes white chocolate, which has become very popular.

Mr. Smith has 20 years of experience in the chocolate industry, and he keeps abreast of all market trends as well as the successes and failures of his competitors. Mr. Smith coordinates the efforts of each functional area through a detailed operational plan.

REPAYMENT ANALYSIS
Primary:

The primary source of repayment is the cash flows of the company. The following figures are in thousands:

	Actual FYE 1991	Actual FYE 1992	Actual FYE 1993	Projected FYE 1994
Accrual Basis:				
Net Profit	($ 26)	$ 23	$ 10	$ 19
Add: Deprec. in COGS	$ 25	$ 25	$ 30	$ 35
Add: Depreciation	$ 10	$ 25	$ 25	$ 29
Add: Amortization	$ 5	$ 5	$ 5	$ 5
Add: Interest Exp.	$ 21	$ 27	$ 36	$ 42
Add: Rent Expense	$100	$100	$110	$110
Add: Charitable Cont.	-0-	-0-	$ 10	$ 10
Less: Gain/Asset sale	-0-	-0-	($ 12)	-0-
Less: Dividends	-0-	($ 5)	($ 10)	($ 6)
TOTAL AVAILABLE	$135	$200	$204	$244

Sample Loan Presentation

	Actual FYE 1991	Actual FYE 1992	Actual FYE 1993	Projected FYE 1994
Cash Basis:				
Net Cash After Oper.	N/A	15	($ 88)	$129
Add: Rent Expense	N/A	$100	$110	$110
Add: Charitable Cont.	N/A	-0-	$ 10	$ 10
Less: Dividends	N/A	($ 5)	($ 10)	($ 6)
TOTAL AVAILABLE	N/A	$110	$ 22	$243

TOTAL PROJECTED DEBT SERVICE:

Annual Payment:	Loan:	Description of payment:
$ 47	$230 Bank Term Note	Monthly principal payments of $2,500 plus interest accrued at 8%.
$ 20	$58 Bank Term Note	Monthly principal and interest payments of $1,657.
$ 86	$500 Commercial Mortgage	Monthly principal payments of $4,167 plus interest accrued at 8%.
$ 12	$150 Line of Credit	Monthly interest only payments at 8%. Assume that the line of credit is fully drawn.
$ 8	$75 Officer Loan	Interest only payments at 10%.
$173	**TOTAL DEBT SERVICE REQUIRED ANNUALLY**	

DEBT SERVICE COVERAGE:

	1991	1992	1993	1994
Accrual Basis:				
Total Accrual Avail.	$135	$200	$204	$244
Total Debt Service	$173	$173	$173	$173
Debt Coverage Ratio	0.78x	1.16x	1.18x	1.41x
Excess/(deficit)	($ 38)	$ 27	$ 31	$ 71

Chapter 10

Cash Basis:
Total Cash Avail.	N/A	$110	$ 22	$243
Total Debt Service	N/A	$173	$173	$173
Debt Coverage Ratio	N/A	0.64x	0.13x	1.40x
Excess/(deficit)	N/A	($ 63)	($151)	$ 70

On an accrual basis, the company shows the ability to service its debts. Debt service coverage is almost 1.20 times in 1992 and 1993. In fact, there is an extra cushion of approximately $30,000 during these years. For 1994 the analyst has projected debt service coverage of 1.41 times.

When cash flows from changes in receivable, payable, inventory, and prepaid/accrual balances are included in the calculation, there is significantly less cash available during the historical periods. The company is unable to service its debt in 1992 and 1993 as measured by the cash basis cash flow. The shortages are $63,000 in 1992 and $151,000 in 1993. For 1994, cash basis debt service coverage is adequate due to projected improvements in turnover ratios/swing factors.

In 1992, receivables rose by $56,000 and inventories rose by $32,000. The increases in these two accounts used a total of $88,000 in cash and were the primary reason for the deficit coverage. Notice that not only sales increases, but also decreases in turnover rates contributed to the use of cash.

Again in 1993, the receivable and inventory balances increased dramatically for a total $227,000 use of cash. Again, receivable and inventory turnover rates decreased. This implies that not only was the $227,000 in cash used to finance increasing sales, but that it was used to finance slower inventory turnover and slower collection of receivables.

In 1993, however, the payables balance also increased for a $58,000 source of cash. The payables

Sample Loan Presentation

increase offsets a portion of the use of cash for receivables and inventory.

The extension of the payables balance in 1993 is a sign of potential trouble. The company's line of credit is fully drawn, but they still need cash. Consequently, the company has extended payables (payables turnover increased), and they have even overdrawn their bank account. The company needs a larger line of credit to avoid this in the future. This is further evidenced by projections which call for short-term borrowings of $110,000 at December 31, 1994.

Secondary:

The secondary source of repayment for the loan is liquidation of collateral. The following values are in thousands:

Loan	Collateral	Book Value	Liquidation Value	Basis
$150 line	Accounts Receivable	$260	$195	75% eligible 12-31-93
	Inventory	$298	$149	50% of book 12-31-93
	Fixed Assets	$131	$-0-	no value taken
	TOTAL	$706	$344	

Loan to liquidation value: 43.6%

Accounts Receivable Aging: (in thousands)

Current	$200	(72%)
31-60 days	$ 30	(11%)
61-90 days	$ 30	(11%)
over 90 days	$ 17	(6%)
TOTAL	$277	

Chapter 10

Tertiary:

The tertiary source of repayment will be enforcement of the personal guarantee.

The guarantor, Mr. Charles Smith, has adjusted net worth of $328,300 and liquid assets of $25,500.

Mr. Smith had personal cash available of $48,550 in 1992 against debt service of $21,344 for a 44.0 percent debt to income ratio.

INCOME STATEMENT ANALYSIS

The most striking trend is the overall growth of the company from 1990 to 1993. Sales have grown due to aggressive marketing by Mr. Smith and the sales team. Word-of-mouth has also spread through candy stores, and increasing numbers of new stores are adding Charlie's Chocolate Company products to their shelves. Mr. Smith expects this growth to continue through 1994. While sales have grown, prices have remained fairly steady in the industry due to competition.

Both the gross profit margin and the operating profit margin (or cushion) improved in 1992, but declined in 1993. The decline in 1993 is attributed to the rapid growth of the company as well as increasing price competition among chocolate suppliers.

BALANCE SHEET ANALYSIS

Working capital appears adequate. As of December 31, 1993, there is a $269,000 cushion between current assets and current liabilities. The current ratio also appears adequate; however, it has declined each year. The quick ratio has fallen below 1:1. The company may, therefore, be reliant upon increased inventory turnover to service short-term debt payments.

Receivables turnover slowed in both 1992 and 1993. The quality of these receivables is reported to be good. Receivables are due from large retailers, "mom and pop" stores, and everything in between. Currently, 6 percent of accounts receivable are 90 or more days past due; bad debt expense was $16,000 in 1993. The company now offers discounts for prompt payment, and management feels that this will improve receivable turnover in the future.

Inventory turnover has remained above 150 days, and it is rising. Goods were held in inventory for an average of 166 days in 1993. The company has recently stocked up on inventory due to anticipated sales growth and supplier discounts. The company realizes the importance of controlling inventory turnover, and this will be a major objective in 1994.

Payables turnover improved in 1992 but slowed to 57 days in 1993 due to cash flow problems. The increased line of credit should alleviate much of this problem.

Debt to worth improved to 5.55 to 1 at December 31, 1992, but increased to 7.60 to 1 at December 31, 1993. (Notice that in 1993 accounts payable, the bank line, and long-term bank debt all increased, while net worth remained exactly the same.)

The high debt to worth is not a matter for serious concern in this case. The company owes $75,000 subordinated debt to Mr. Smith. When this debt is treated as equity, the ratio becomes 3.64 to 1 at December 31, 1993.

INDUSTRY OUTLOOK

The chocolate industry has become increasingly competitive over the past few years. Prices have remained steady due to competition and lower raw materials costs. Charlie's Chocolate Company's major competitors include local, regional, and national producers of premium chocolates.

Chapter 10

The current level of competition is expected to continue. Smaller producers are expected to be acquired by larger producers seeking economies of scale. Smaller producers which are not acquired are expected to fail due to heavy competition and increasing equipment costs.

ENVIRONMENTAL CONCERNS

There are no environmental concerns related to this loan request.

COMMERCIAL LOAN ANALYSIS— PROCESS RENEWAL

Presentation of the loan request to the committee is the final step in the commercial loan analysis process. This process is renewed when the borrower applies for additional debt, when the current loans mature, when repayment problems arise, or when a regularly scheduled review occurs.

WORKSHEETS

Worksheets

Balance Sheets—Assets

Cash		
Accounts Receivable—Trade		
Less: Allowance for Doubtful Accounts		
Accounts Receivable—Other		
NET ACCOUNTS RECEIVABLE		
Raw Materials		
Work in Progress		
Finished Goods		
Other Inventory		
TOTAL INVENTORY		
Accounts/Notes Receivable—Current		
Income Taxes Receivable		
Prepaid Expenses—Current		
Other Current Assets		
TOTAL CURRENT ASSETS		
Land		
Buildings		
Furniture and Fixtures		
Machinery and Equipment		
Leashold Improvements		
Transportation Equipment		
Capitalized Leases		
Other Fixed Assets		
Less: Accumulated Depreciation		
NET FIXED ASSETS		

Balance Sheets—Assets (continued)

Accounts/Notes Receivable—Non-Current		
Accounts/Notes Receivable—Officers/Stockholders		
Investments		
Prepaid Expenses—Non-Current		
Cash Value of Life Insurance		
Other Non-Current Assets		
Intangible Assets		
TOTAL NON-CURRENT ASSETS		
TOTAL ASSETS		

Worksheets

Balance Sheets—Assets

Cash		
Accounts Receivable—Trade		
Less: Allowance for Doubtful Accounts		
Accounts Receivable—Other		
NET ACCOUNTS RECEIVABLE		
Raw Materials		
Work in Progress		
Finished Goods		
Other Inventory		
TOTAL INVENTORY		
Accounts/Notes Receivable—Current		
Income Taxes Receivable		
Prepaid Expenses—Current		
Other Current Assets		
TOTAL CURRENT ASSETS		
Land		
Buildings		
Furniture and Fixtures		
Machinery and Equipment		
Leashold Improvements		
Transportation Equipment		
Capitalized Leases		
Other Fixed Assets		
Less: Accumulated Depreciation		
NET FIXED ASSETS		

Balance Sheets—Assets (continued)

Accounts/Notes Receivable—Non-Current		
Accounts/Notes Receivable—Officers/Stockholders		
Investments		
Prepaid Expenses—Non-Current		
Cash Value of Life Insurance		
Other Non-Current Assets		
Intangible Assets		
TOTAL NON-CURRENT ASSETS		
TOTAL ASSETS		

Worksheets

Balance Sheets—Assets

Cash		
Accounts Receivable—Trade		
Less: Allowance for Doubtful Accounts		
Accounts Receivable—Other		
NET ACCOUNTS RECEIVABLE		
Raw Materials		
Work in Progress		
Finished Goods		
Other Inventory		
TOTAL INVENTORY		
Accounts/Notes Receivable—Current		
Income Taxes Receivable		
Prepaid Expenses—Current		
Other Current Assets		
TOTAL CURRENT ASSETS		
Land		
Buildings		
Furniture and Fixtures		
Machinery and Equipment		
Leashold Improvements		
Transportation Equipment		
Capitalized Leases		
Other Fixed Assets		
Less: Accumulated Depreciation		
NET FIXED ASSETS		

Balance Sheets—Assets (continued)

Accounts/Notes Receivable—Non-Current		
Accounts/Notes Receivable—Officers/Stockholders		
Investments		
Prepaid Expenses—Non-Current		
Cash Value of Life Insurance		
Other Non-Current Assets		
Intangible Assets		
TOTAL NON-CURRENT ASSETS		
TOTAL ASSETS		

Worksheets

Balance Sheets—Liabilities/Equity

Overdraft		
Notes Payable—Short Term		
Current Portion of Long-Term Debt		
Accounts Payable—Trade		
Accounts Payable—Other		
Accounts/Notes Payable—Officers/ Stockholders		
Income Taxes Payable		
Other Current Liabilities		
Accured Interest		
Dividends Payable		
Accrued Taxes		
Other Accruals		
TOTAL ACCRUED LIABILITIES		
TOTAL CURRENT LIABILITIES		
Long-Term Debt		
Accounts/Notes Payable—Officers/ Stockholders		
Deferred Income Tax		
Deferred Income		
Other Non-Current Liability		
Subordinate Debt-Liability		
TOTAL NON-CURRENT LIABILITIES		
TOTAL LIABILITIES		

Worksheets

Balance Sheets—Libabilities/Equity (continued)

Common Stock		
Additional Paid in Capital		
Less Treasury Stock		
Retained Earnings		
Other Equity		
TOTAL EQUITY		
TOTAL LIABILITIES AND NET WORTH		

Worksheets

Balance Sheets—Liabilities/Equity

Overdraft		
Notes Payable—Short Term		
Current Portion of Long-Term Debt		
Accounts Payable—Trade		
Accounts Payable—Other		
Accounts/Notes Payable—Officers/ Stockholders		
Income Taxes Payable		
Other Current Liabilities		
Accured Interest		
Dividends Payable		
Accrued Taxes		
Other Accruals		
TOTAL ACCRUED LIABILITIES		
TOTAL CURRENT LIABILITIES		
Long-Term Debt		
Accounts/Notes Payable—Officers/ Stockholders		
Deferred Income Tax		
Deferred Income		
Other Non-Current Liability		
Subordinate Debt-Liability		
TOTAL NON-CURRENT LIABILITIES		
TOTAL LIABILITIES		

Balance Sheets—Libabilities/Equity
(continued)

Common Stock		
Additional Paid in Capital		
Less Treasury Stock		
Retained Earnings		
Other Equity		
TOTAL EQUITY		
TOTAL LIABILITIES AND NET WORTH		

Worksheets

Balance Sheets—Liabilities/Equity

Overdraft		
Notes Payable—Short Term		
Current Portion of Long-Term Debt		
Accounts Payable—Trade		
Accounts Payable—Other		
Accounts/Notes Payable—Officers/Stockholders		
Income Taxes Payable		
Other Current Liabilities		
Accured Interest		
Dividends Payable		
Accrued Taxes		
Other Accruals		
TOTAL ACCRUED LIABILITIES		
TOTAL CURRENT LIABILITIES		
Long-Term Debt		
Accounts/Notes Payable—Officers/Stockholders		
Deferred Income Tax		
Deferred Income		
Other Non-Current Liability		
Subordinate Debt-Liability		
TOTAL NON-CURRENT LIABILITIES		
TOTAL LIABILITIES		

Balance Sheets—Libabilities/Equity
(continued)

Common Stock		
Additional Paid in Capital		
Less Treasury Stock		
Retained Earnings		
Other Equity		
TOTAL EQUITY		
TOTAL LIABILITIES AND NET WORTH		

Worksheets

Income Statement

Revenue		
Less: Returns and Allowances		
Less: Discounts		
Other Revenue		
NET REVENUE		
Cost of Goods Sold		
Cost of Goods Sold—Other		
Cost of Goods Solds—Deprectiation		
TOTAL COST OF GOODS SOLD		
GROSS PROFIT		
Operating Expenses		
Officers Salary		
Rent Expense		
Bad Debt Expense		
Other Operating Expense		
Depreciation Expense		
Amortization Expense		
TOTAL OPERATING EXPENSE		
OPERATING PROFIT		
Interest Expense		
Interest Income		
Other Expense		
Gain (Loss) on Sale of Assets		
Income Tax		
Extraordinary Gain (Loss)		

Income Statement (continued)

Dividends		
Accounting Change		
Prior Period Adjustment		
Change in Retained Earnings		
NET CHANGE IN EQUITY		

Worksheets

Income Statement

Revenue		
Less: Returns and Allowances		
Less: Discounts		
Other Revenue		
NET REVENUE		
Cost of Goods Sold		
Cost of Goods Sold—Other		
Cost of Goods Solds—Deprectiation		
TOTAL COST OF GOODS SOLD		
GROSS PROFIT		
Operating Expenses		
Officers Salary		
Rent Expense		
Bad Debt Expense		
Other Operating Expense		
Depreciation Expense		
Amortization Expense		
TOTAL OPERATING EXPENSE		
OPERATING PROFIT		
Interest Expense		
Interest Income		
Other Expense		
Gain (Loss) on Sale of Assets		
Income Tax		
Extraordinary Gain (Loss)		

Income Statement (continued)

Dividends		
Accounting Change		
Prior Period Adjustment		
Change in Retained Earnings		
NET CHANGE IN EQUITY		

Worksheets

Income Statement

Revenue		
Less: Returns and Allowances		
Less: Discounts		
Other Revenue		
NET REVENUE		
Cost of Goods Sold		
Cost of Goods Sold—Other		
Cost of Goods Solds—Deprectiation		
TOTAL COST OF GOODS SOLD		
GROSS PROFIT		
Operating Expenses		
Officers Salary		
Rent Expense		
Bad Debt Expense		
Other Operating Expense		
Depreciation Expense		
Amortization Expense		
TOTAL OPERATING EXPENSE		
OPERATING PROFIT		
Interest Expense		
Interest Income		
Other Expense		
Gain (Loss) on Sale of Assets		
Income Tax		
Extraordinary Gain (Loss)		

Worksheets

Income Statement (continued)

Dividends		
Accounting Change		
Prior Period Adjustment		
Change in Retained Earnings		
NET CHANGE IN EQUITY		

Worksheets

Statement of Cash Flows

Net Revenue		
Changes in Receivables		
CASH FROM REVENUE		
Cost of Goods Sold		
Change in Inventories		
Change in Payables		
CASH PRODUCTION COSTS		
GROSS CASH PROFIT		
Operating Expense		
Change in Prepaids		
Change in Accruals		
CASH OPERATING EXPENSE		
CASH AFTER OPERATIONS		
Miscellaneous Cash Income (Expense)		
Cash Income Tax Paid		
NET CASH AFTER OPERATIONS		
Cash Interest Expense		
NET CASH INCOME		
Current Portion of Long-Term Debt		
CASH AFTER DEBT AMORTIZATION		

Worksheets

Statement of Cash Flows (continued)

Capital Expenditures—Tangible		
Investments		
FINANCING SURPLUS (DEFICIT)		
Change in Short-Term Debt		
Change in Long-Term Debt		
TOTAL EXTERNAL FINANCING		
Cash After Financing		
Actual Change In Cash		

Worksheets

Statement of Cash Flows

Net Revenue		
Changes in Receivables		
CASH FROM REVENUE		
Cost of Goods Sold		
Change in Inventories		
Change in Payables		
CASH PRODUCTION COSTS		
GROSS CASH PROFIT		
Operating Expense		
Change in Prepaids		
Change in Accruals		
CASH OPERATING EXPENSE		
CASH AFTER OPERATIONS		
Miscellaneous Cash Income (Expense)		
Cash Income Tax Paid		
NET CASH AFTER OPERATIONS		
Cash Interest Expense		
NET CASH INCOME		
Current Portion of Long-Term Debt		
CASH AFTER DEBT AMORTIZATION		

Statement of Cash Flows (continued)

Capital Expenditures—Tangible		
Investments		
FINANCING SURPLUS (DEFICIT)		
Change in Short-Term Debt		
Change in Long-Term Debt		
TOTAL EXTERNAL FINANCING		
Cash After Financing		
Actual Change In Cash		

Worksheets

Statement of Cash Flows

Net Revenue		
Changes in Receivables		
CASH FROM REVENUE		
Cost of Goods Sold		
Change in Inventories		
Change in Payables		
CASH PRODUCTION COSTS		
GROSS CASH PROFIT		
Operating Expense		
Change in Prepaids		
Change in Accruals		
CASH OPERATING EXPENSE		
CASH AFTER OPERATIONS		
Miscellaneous Cash Income (Expense)		
Cash Income Tax Paid		
NET CASH AFTER OPERATIONS		
Cash Interest Expense		
NET CASH INCOME		
Current Portion of Long-Term Debt		
CASH AFTER DEBT AMORTIZATION		

Statement of Cash Flows (continued)

Capital Expenditures—Tangible		
Investments		
FINANCING SURPLUS (DEFICIT)		
Change in Short-Term Debt		
Change in Long-Term Debt		
TOTAL EXTERNAL FINANCING		
Cash After Financing		
Actual Change In Cash		

Worksheets

Financial Ratios

Total Current Assets
− Total Current Liabilities
WORKING CAPITAL

$$\text{CURRENT RATIO} = \frac{\text{Total Current Assets}}{\text{Total Current Liabilities}}$$

$$\text{QUICK RATIO} = \frac{\text{Cash Plus Receivables}}{\text{Total Current Liabilities}}$$

$$\text{RECEIVABLES TURNOVER} = \frac{\text{Net Revenue}}{\text{Trade Receivables}}$$

$$\text{RECEIVABLES DAYS} = \frac{365}{\text{Receivables Turnover}}$$

$$\text{INVENTORY TURNOVER} = \frac{\text{Cost of Sales}}{\text{Inventory}}$$

$$\text{INVENTORY DAYS} = \frac{365}{\text{Inventory Turnover}}$$

$$\text{PAYABLES TURNOVER} = \frac{\text{Cost of Sales}}{\text{Trade Payables}}$$

$$\text{PAYABLES DAYS} = \frac{365}{\text{Payables Turnover}}$$

$$\text{DEBT TO WORTH} = \frac{\text{Total Liabilities}}{\text{Net Worth}}$$

Worksheets

Financial Ratios (continued)

$$\text{SENIOR DEBT TO WORTH} = \frac{\text{Senior Debt}}{\text{Tangible Net Worth}}$$

$$\text{EBIT / INTREST RATIO} = \frac{\text{EBIT}}{\text{Interest Expense}}$$

$$\text{CASH FLOW / CPLTD} = \frac{\text{Net Profit + Depreciation, Amortization, Depletion Cash Flow}}{\text{Current Portion of Long–Term Debt}}$$

$$\text{GROSS PROFIT MARGIN} = \frac{\text{Gross Profit}}{\text{Net Revenue}}$$

$$\text{OPERATING PROFIT MARGIN} = \frac{\text{Operating Profit}}{\text{Net Revenue}}$$

$$\text{NET PROFIT MARGIN} = \frac{\text{Net Income}}{\text{Net Revenue}}$$

$$\text{REVENUE TO TOTAL ASSETS} = \frac{\text{Net Revenue}}{\text{Total Assets}}$$

$$\text{REVENUE TO FIXED ASSETS} = \frac{\text{Net Revenue}}{\text{Net Fixed Assets}}$$

$$\text{REVENUE TO WORKING CAPITAL} = \frac{\text{Net Revenue}}{\text{Working Capital}}$$

Worksheets

Debt Service Coverage Analysis

Net Income		
Add: Depreciation/Amortization		
Add: Rents Paid to Owners		
Less: Dividends/Withdrawals		
Add: Officer Salaries		
Add: Extraordinary Losses		
Subtract: Extraordinary Gains		
Add: Loss os Sale of Assets		
Less: Gain on Sale of Assets		
Add: Pension/Charitable Contributions		
Other Adjustments		
TOTAL ACCRUAL BASIS CASH AVAILABLE DEBT SERVICE COVERAGE RATIO EXCESS/(DEFICIT)		
Net Cash after Operations		
Add: Rents Paid to Owners		
Less: Dividends/Withdrawals		
Add: Officer Salaries		
Add: Extraordinary Losses		
Subtract: Extraordinary Gains		
Add: Pension/Charitable Contributions		
Other Adjustments		
TOTAL CASH BASIS CASH AVAILABLE DEBT SERVICE COVERAGE RATIO EXCESS/(DEFICIT)		

Worksheets

Debt Service Coverage Analysis
(continued)

Debt Service:		
1.		
2.		
3.		
4.		
5.		
6.		
7.		
8.		
TOTAL ANNUAL DEBT SERVICE		

Worksheets

Debt Service Coverage Analysis

Net Income		
Add: Depreciation/Amortization		
Add: Rents Paid to Owners		
Less: Dividends/Withdrawals		
Add: Officer Salaries		
Add: Extraordinary Losses		
Subtract: Extraordinary Gains		
Add: Loss os Sale of Assets		
Less: Gain on Sale of Assets		
Add: Pension/Charitable Contributions		
Other Adjustments		
TOTAL ACCRUAL BASIS CASH AVAILABLE DEBT SERVICE COVERAGE RATIO EXCESS/(DEFICIT)		
Net Cash after Operations		
Add: Rents Paid to Owners		
Less: Dividends/Withdrawals		
Add: Officer Salaries		
Add: Extraordinary Losses		
Subtract: Extraordinary Gains		
Add: Pension/Charitable Contributions		
Other Adjustments		
TOTAL CASH BASIS CASH AVAILABLE DEBT SERVICE COVERAGE RATIO EXCESS/(DEFICIT)		

Worksheets

Debt Service Coverage Analysis
(continued)

Debt Service:		
1.		
2.		
3.		
4.		
5.		
6.		
7.		
8.		
TOTAL ANNUAL DEBT SERVICE		

Worksheets

Debt Service Coverage Analysis

Net Income		
Add: Depreciation/Amortization		
Add: Rents Paid to Owners		
Less: Dividends/Withdrawals		
Add: Officer Salaries		
Add: Extraordinary Losses		
Subtract: Extraordinary Gains		
Add: Loss os Sale of Assets		
Less: Gain on Sale of Assets		
Add: Pension/Charitable Contributions		
Other Adjustments		
TOTAL ACCRUAL BASIS CASH AVAILABLE DEBT SERVICE COVERAGE RATIO EXCESS/(DEFICIT)		
Net Cash after Operations		
Add: Rents Paid to Owners		
Less: Dividends/Withdrawals		
Add: Officer Salaries		
Add: Extraordinary Losses		
Subtract: Extraordinary Gains		
Add: Pension/Charitable Contributions		
Other Adjustments		
TOTAL CASH BASIS CASH AVAILABLE DEBT SERVICE COVERAGE RATIO EXCESS/(DEFICIT)		

Debt Service Coverage Analysis
(continued)

Debt Service:		
1.		
2.		
3.		
4.		
5.		
6.		
7.		
8.		
TOTAL ANNUAL DEBT SERVICE		

Worksheets

Personal Financial Statement Analysis

Cash		
U.S. Government Securities		
Listed Securities		
Other Liquid Assets		
TOTAL LIQUID ASSETS		
Unlisted Securities		
Retirement/IRA		
Inside Business Equity*		
Accounts/Loan Receivable		
Inside Loans Receivable*		
Cash Value of Life Insurance		
Residence		
Real Estate*		
Inside Real Estate*		
Vehicles		
Personal property-good		
Personal property-questionable*		
Other Assets		
TOTAL ASSETS		
Unsecured Loans		
Loans Secured by Liquid Assets		
Loans Secured by Life Insurance		
Residental Mortgage		
Real Estate Mortgages		
Loans Secured by Vehicles		
Other Secured Loans		
Credit Card Debt		

Personal Financial Statement Analysis
(continued)

Taxes Payable		
Other Liabilities		
TOTAL LIABILITIES		
TOTAL NET WORTH		
*ADJUSTED NET WORTH		
LIQUID ASSET EQUITY		
LIFE INSURANCE EQUITY		
RESIDENCE EQUITY		
VEHICLE EQUITY		
*Assets marked with star above are excluded from calculation of adjusted net worth.		

Worksheets

Personal Financial Statement Analysis

Cash		
U.S. Government Securities		
Listed Securities		
Other Liquid Assets		
TOTAL LIQUID ASSETS		
Unlisted Securities		
Retirement/IRA		
Inside Business Equity*		
Accounts/Loan Receivable		
Inside Loans Receivable*		
Cash Value of Life Insurance		
Residence		
Real Estate*		
Inside Real Estate*		
Vehicles		
Personal property-good		
Personal property-questionable*		
Other Assets		
TOTAL ASSETS		
Unsecured Loans		
Loans Secured by Liquid Assets		
Loans Secured by Life Insurance		
Residental Mortgage		
Real Estate Mortgages		
Loans Secured by Vehicles		
Other Secured Loans		
Credit Card Debt		

Worksheets

Personal Financial Statement Analysis
(continued)

Taxes Payable		
Other Liabilities		
TOTAL LIABILITIES		
TOTAL NET WORTH		
*ADJUSTED NET WORTH		
LIQUID ASSET EQUITY		
LIFE INSURANCE EQUITY		
RESIDENCE EQUITY		
VEHICLE EQUITY		
*Assets marked with star above are excluded from calculation of adjusted net worth.		

Worksheets

Personal Financial Statement Analysis

Cash		
U.S. Government Securities		
Listed Securities		
Other Liquid Assets		
TOTAL LIQUID ASSETS		
Unlisted Securities		
Retirement/IRA		
Inside Business Equity*		
Accounts/Loan Receivable		
Inside Loans Receivable*		
Cash Value of Life Insurance		
Residence		
Real Estate*		
Inside Real Estate*		
Vehicles		
Personal property-good		
Personal property-questionable*		
Other Assets		
TOTAL ASSETS		
Unsecured Loans		
Loans Secured by Liquid Assets		
Loans Secured by Life Insurance		
Residental Mortgage		
Real Estate Mortgages		
Loans Secured by Vehicles		
Other Secured Loans		
Credit Card Debt		

Personal Financial Statement Analysis
(continued)

Taxes Payable		
Other Liabilities		
TOTAL LIABILITIES		
TOTAL NET WORTH		
*ADJUSTED NET WORTH		
LIQUID ASSET EQUITY		
LIFE INSURANCE EQUITY		
RESIDENCE EQUITY		
VEHICLE EQUITY		
*Assets marked with star above are excluded from calculation of adjusted net worth.		

SOURCES

Alonso, Juan; Bessemer, Pat; Levine, Eris; and Strischek, Dev. "Evaluating Personal Financial Statements: How to Calculate Adjusted Net Worth." *Commercial Lending Review*. Fall 1989. pp. 3–17.

Clifton, Gunderson & Co., Certified Public Accountants & Consultants. *Understanding Financial Statements; Compilations, Reviews, and Audits, What's the Difference*. 1992.

Financial Proformas, Inc. *CAL Cash Flow Dynamics*. Rex Beach & Associates, Inc. 1986.

First of America Bank Corporation. *Instructions for Preparation of Commercial Loan Applications under the June 1991 Revised FOABC standardized format*. June 1991.

Illinois Department of Commerce and Community Affairs—Office of Urban Assistance. *A Business Plan Outline*. June 1989.

McKinley, John E.; Johnson, Robert L.; Downey, Gerald R., Jr.; Zimmerman, Charles S.; and Bloom, Michael D. *Analyzing Financial Statements*. American Bankers Association. 1984.

Morsman, Edgar M., Jr. "Commercial Loan Structuring." *The Journal of Commercial Bank Lending*. November 1991. pp. 25–42.

Potter, Scott. "Analyzing the Self-Employed Borrower," Parts A & B. *Financial Seminars, Inc*. 1993.

Robert Morris Associates. *Annual Statement Studies*. 1992. pp. 9–15.

Robert Morris Associates and Wells Fargo & Company. *Uniform Credit Analysis—Preliminary Materials*. 1988, 1990, 1992.

INDEX

A

ABI, 99
Accounts Receivable, 19, 29, 57, 111
Accounts Payable, 20, 57
Accrual Basis Cash Flow, 44-48, 51, 54, 108-109
Accrued Interest, 3, 8
Acid Test, 30
Activity Ratios, 31-33
Additional Support, 74, 78
Adjusted Net Worth, 73-75, 78, 112
Advance Formula, 104, 106
Alimony, 89
Amortization, 9, 21, 44, 50, 98
Asset Based Lending, 97
Assets, 6-8
  current, 7, 29, 39
  non-current, 7
  spreading, 7, 19-20
Assignment, 100
Audit, 6

B

Bad Debt Expense, 9, 21, 38
Balloon, 98
Breakeven Occupancy Percentage, 38
Breakeven Ratios, 37-38
Bridge Loan, 96
Business Assets, 100
Business Plan, 59-61, 108

C

Capital Expenditures, 54
Capital Requirements, 12
Cash Account, 6, 19
Cash Available Calculation, 9, 44-48, 109-110
  summary, 52
Cash Basis Cash Flow, 48-50, 51, 52, 54, 110
Cash Flow analysis, 43-58
  business, 44-48, 108
  personal, 79-93
Cash Flow from Operations, 44
Cash Flow Statement, 7, 8, 49, 50
Cash Flow/CMLTD Ratio, 34-35
Cash Value of Life Insurance, 74, 78
Ceiling, 98
Charitable Contributions, 10, 21, 47, 49
Clean-up Period, 104
Collateral, 43, 97, 106, 111
Commercial Installment Note, 96

Index

Commercial Real Estate Mortgage, 96
Competition, 112, 113, 114
Compiled Financial Statements, 6, 14, 19
Cost of Goods Sold, 9, 21
Coverage Ratios, 57
Cross-Collateralization, 100
Cross-Default, 104
Crowe, Chizek & Company, 5
Current Assets, 7, 30
Current Liabilities, 8, 30–26
Current Portion of Long-Term Debt, 8, 20
Current Ratio, 30-31, 39, 112
Cushion, 30, 35, 39

D

Debt Service, 37, 48, 54, 90, 109
Debt Service Coverage Analysis, 9, 43-58, 56, 109-112
Debt Service Coverage Ratio, 37, 44, 48, 104, 109
Debt to Income Ratio, 90
Debt to Worth Ratio, 7, 33, 40, 113
Deficit Cash Available, 48, 90
Depreciation, 9, 20, 21, 35, 45, 50
Direct Expenses, 9
Discretionary Income and Expenses, 47
Dividends, 9, 11, 21, 22, 46, 49, 82, 109

E

EBIT/Interest Ratio, 34
Efficiency Ratios, 35-37, 40-41
Employee Advances, 7
Employee Loans, 19
Evergreen Loan, 97
Expense to Sales Ratios, 35-37
Expiration, 98
Extraordinary Gains and Losses, 10, 46, 49

F

FAMAS, 5
Financial Proformas, Inc., 5, 22
Financial Statement, 5, 19-22
 types, 5–6
First Mortgage, 99, 102
Fixed Assets, 10, 20, 37, 54
Fixed Rate, 98
Floor, 98
Franchise Fees, 7
Fundamental Factors, 51

G

Gain on Sale of Assets, 10, 21, 46, 50, 54
General Business Security Agreement, 100
Goodwill, 7, 20, 34
Gross Profit Margin, 35, 40, 112
Guarantee, 82, 102-103

I

Impacts Upon Cash Flow, 52
Income Statement, Spreading, 5, 8-10, 21-22
Income Taxes, 10, 80, 91
Individual Retirement Account (IRA), 75, 82, 91
Industry Averages, 11, 41
Intangible Assets, 7, 20
Interest Expense, 9, 21, 45, 50, 81
Interest Income, 10, 89, 92
Interest Payable, 7, 20
Interest Rate, 64, 98
Inventory, 7, 19, 29, 31, 39, 57, 58, 102
 Life Cycle, 102
Inventory Days, 32, 39
Inventory Turnover, 32, 39, 40, 57, 65
IRA, 75, 82, 91

Index

L

Leasehold Improvements, 7
Letter of Credit, 7, 95-96
Leverage, 33, 37, 40
Liabilities, 8
  current, 8, 39
  non-current, 8
  spreading, 8, 20-21
Life Cycle Value of Inventory, 102
Limited Guarantee, 103
Line of Credit, 65, 95, 97, 106, 109
Liquidity Ratios, 29-31, 39-40
Loan Fees, 7
Loan Payment, 98
Loan Presentation, 105-114
Loan Pricing, 98-99
Loan Structuring, 95-104
Loan to Liquidation Value, 101, 111
Loan to Value, 101
Long-Term Assets, 7
Long-Term Debt, 8, 12, 20, 29
Loss on Sale of Assets, 10, 46, 50, 54

M

Management, 59-61, 108
Matching, 12
Maturity, 97
Mission, 59, 108
Mortgage, 96, 99

N

Negative Pledge, 102
Net Cash after Operations, 49, 53
Net Profit, 36, 44
Net Profit Margin, 36
Non-Current Liabilities, 8
Notes Payable, 8, 20
  officers and stockholders, 8

O

Officer Loans, 7, 109
Officer's Compensation, 9, 64
Officer's Salary, 21, 46, 49, 79
Operating Expenses, 9, 10, 21
Operating Profit Margin, 35, 40, 112
Operating Ratios, 35-37, 40-41
Overdrafts, 6, 19, 29

P

Payables Days, 33
Payables Turnover, 32-33, 40, 65, 111
Payment, 98
Pension Plan Contributions, 10, 47, 49
Permanent Working Capital Loan, 97
Personal Cash Flow Analysis, 79-93
Personal Financial Statement, 73-78
Points, 99
Prepaid Expenses, 7, 19
Prepaid Interest, 7
Prepayment Penalty, 99
Pricing, 60, 98-99, 106
Primary Source or Repayment, 44, 106
Principal and Interest Payment, 98
Principal Plus Interest Payment, 98
Profitability Ratios, 35-37, 40-41
Projections, 54, 59, 63-71

Q

Qualified Audit, 6
Quick Ratio, 30, 39, 112

R

Ratios, 29-41
Receivables Days, 31-32
Receivables Turnover, 31, 32, 39, 65
Rent Expense, 9, 21, 45, 49
Repayment History, 43
Retained Earnings, 21, 22
  Adjustments, 11, 22
Return on Assets, 36, 37
Return on Equity, 36, 37
Revenues, 9, 10, 21, 31, 37-38

Index

Reviewed Financial Statements, 6
ROA, 36, 37
Robert Morris Associates, 11, 30, 36
ROE, 36, 37
Royalties, 81

S

Sales, 9, 21, 36, 37, 39, 64, 71, 110
Sales to Net Fixed Assets, 37, 41
Sales to Total Assets Ratio, 36, 41
Sales to Working Capital Ratio, 37, 41
Seasonal Loan, 96-97
Second Mortgage, 99, 102
Secondary Source of Repayment, 111
Senior Debt to Worth Ratio, 8, 34
Sensitivity Analysis, 63, 71
Short-Term Working Capital Line of Credit, 12, 106
Single-Payment Note, 95
Source of Cash, 52-53
Spreading, 5-6, 19-22
Start-up Costs, 7
Statement of Cash Flows, 50-51
Stockholder Loans, 7, 19
Subordinated Debt, 8, 20, 40, 91
Subordination, 9, 103
Swing Factors, 51, 52, 110

T

Tax Returns, 80-92
Term, 98
Term Loan, 97
Total Cash Available, 10, 44-48, 80
Total Debt Service, 48, 80, 90, 109, 110
Total Liquid Assets, 73, 75
Traditional Cash Flow, 44-45
Trends, 10, 38, 112
Triple Net Basis, 3, 107
Turbo Fast, 5, 22-27, 66-70
Turnover Ratios, 31-33, 39-40, 58, 65, 110

U

UCC, 100
Unqualified Audit, 6
Use of Cash, 52-53

V

Variable Rate, 98

W

Withdrawals, 11, 46, 49, 82
Working Capital, 12, 30, 39, 97, 112

About the Author

Kenneth R. Pirok is currently a Credit Analyst at First Midwest Bank/Danville, N.A. in Danville, Illinois. He is responsible for performing commercial loan analysis and administration and for providing analysis training to the lending staff.

He graduated from the University of Illinois with a Bachelor of Science degree in Finance, and he was previously employed as a Credit Analyst at First of America Bank-Northeast Illinois, N.A. in Libertyville, Illinois.

He has also written an article about the use of committees for commercial lending decisions which appeared in the *Journal of Commercial Lending* in February 1993. His plans for the future include pursuit of an MBA degree and organization of a credit department/commercial analysis newsletter.